W9-AGP-193

SHOOT FOR THE PIN

SHOOT FOR THE PIN

The Memoirs of

Francis Joseph Callahan, Jr.

Printed by

Presstige Printing

4551 Arnold Avenue
Naples, Florida 34104

SHOOT FOR THE PIN
Memoirs of Francis Joseph Callahan, Jr.

Printed by Presstige Printing

© 1999 by Francis Joseph Callahan, Jr.

International Standard Book Number
0-9674128-0-3

Printed in the United States of America

ALL RIGHTS RESERVED

TABLE OF CONTENTS

ILLUSTRATIONS

Foreword

I have written this for my children, grandchildren and generations to come. But specifically for my children: Joe, Connie and Tim. Although I don't often say it, I am tremendously proud of all three. My hope is that in reading this they will understand what I was doing during the time they were growing up. Much of what I want them to know they were too young to understand while it happened and at other times, they were too busy or I was too busy.

To a great extent what I have accomplished has been because I was proud of my father and tried to be as good as he was. I hope my children are proud of me. Perhaps in reading these memoirs they will look more kindly on the times I was away from them, busy with my Naval career and building Swagelok Corporation. (And yes, I did play some golf.)

I believe in reading the following pages one can glean some of the important lessons of life. Growing up in a solid, Irish-Catholic neighborhood of Lima, Ohio, my early years exemplified the Latin phrase, *mens sana in corpore sano*. A sound mind in a sound body. I excelled at academics and played all sports. This is an important balance. I have always encouraged my children, and now my grandchildren, in these two aspects of their lives. Sports and academics are equally important. Neither should be neglected.

The next phase was as a midshipman at the Naval Academy. I received more than just a solid academic degree. I learned about DUTY, HONOR and the PROUD TRADITION of the UNITED STATES NAVY. The network of friends that was forged in the classroom and on the parade field at Annapolis could not be equaled anywhere else.

For our 50th reunion in 1995 I was instrumental in starting the fund drive for a $1 million contribution to the Naval Academy Endowment Fund. Each class is now challenged to raise a million dollars to commemorate their 50th reunion.

When I consider, *who is Joe Callahan,* of course I am a husband and father. But near the top I am proud to be a submariner. That was my selected field as I graduated from the Academy on June 6, 1945 near the end of World War II. I feel very strongly about our submarine force and the type of people who serve there. During the war the U.S. Submarine Force composed about 50,000 men including staffs and back-up personnel. This represented only 1.6% of the U.S. Navy but accounted for a staggering 55% of Japan's maritime losses. Of our 288 submarines in World War II we lost in combat 52 submarines and the 3500 men who manned them. Our submarine forces were small but potent, sinking 1,113 Japanese ships representing about five million tons of Japanese shipping. This played a great role in winning the war.

A generally unknown factor in our winning the cold war has been the dedication and sacrifice of the Fleet Ballistic Missile (FBM) Submarine Force. After World War II the Soviets made their submarine force the centerpiece of their naval expansion as well as their primary strategic nuclear force. With each advance the Soviets made we countered with even quieter submarines that went deeper and faster. They were forced to spend enormous resources in an attempt to achieve parity, finally bankrupting the country. Submariners of the FBM submarines have been the unsung heroes of the cold war, making over 3,000 strategic nuclear deterrent patrols since 1960. They were away from their families about 50% of the time. Their sacrifice has been great and largely unnoticed by most Americans.

One of the things that made the submarine force so potent,

compared to other branches of the armed forces, was the ability to select crewmembers. If an officer or enlisted man were assigned to submarine duty and was not ideally suited for the job, it was easy to get him transferred back to the surface fleet. He was simply deemed psychologically unfit for submarines. This was a great advantage to the submarine force and an important lesson that I later carried over to business.

The last part of my active Naval career, August 1954 to January 1958, was working for Admiral H. G. Rickover. He was a great man and had a great impact on my life. However, those who worked closely with him can attest to some of his foibles. I have honestly laid out my own experiences. You can draw your own conclusions.

In August 1957 at age 34, I made a critical assessment of where I was and where I wanted to go. It is an important life lesson to be willing to face reality and to seize opportunities. In 1957 I made the assessment that no amount of competence or productivity on my part would be rewarded with my desired advancement in my Naval career. As an EDO, I could not return to line duty on submarines and I had no place else to go. As much as I loved the Navy I had to face the hard facts of reality. Therefore I resigned to pursue a corporate challenge. My resignation was accepted provided I would stay until January 1958 to train my replacement.

With Swagelok I was able to apply the lessons I had learned as a submariner. As a young submarine officer I remember having the feeling that my crew would not let me down because they did not want me to get into trouble with the Captain. Morale was always high on a submarine. There were important lessons that I brought to bear in building sales and production at Swagelok. For example I kept our plant size small on the model of a 100 crew submarine rather than like the large battleships.

That way the plant manager, like the sub commanding officer, could know the personality and background of each employee. In chapters seven and eight you will see how we used those principles to grow from about $2 million to well over $600 million as a private company. The key is quality. Like in the submarine force we insisted on quality people. In our product lines we became the industry standards because of our quality products.

In the chapter on Entrepreneurship I recount some of my adventures as a venture capitalist. Sure there were some losses. But one particular investment of $100,000 became worth $40 million. While building Swagelok I was invited to serve on the Board of Directors of other corporations. I learned that the logic we applied at our business was not as common as I had expected. Many other businesses were simply not operated very well. This led me to the correct conclusion that large profits could be had in buying and improving other companies.

Chapter ten concerns one of the most important lessons to learn in life. It is important to give. My philanthropic activities began with my involvement with my son's activities. Joe was in the Boy Scouts and that became my first fund raising activity. That has led to my being Chairman of the current $225 million capital campaign for the Cleveland Clinic.

Chapter eleven is the fun chapter. Although, let me quickly note, it has consisted of only 0.6% of my life, less than 9 minutes a day, golf has provided an outstanding amount of relaxation and friendship. I have played well over 100 courses around the world. Often before hiring a key employee or distributor I would arrange a golf game. You can determine a lot about a person's character by their performance on the golf course. Also at Swagelok we have competition among the corporate leagues which helps build company morale. Being very competitive I was able to improve on my score and achieve six hole-in-ones. I only shot under par once but that was at a critical time. It helped our team win third place in the Honda Pro-AM in 1993.

I can't close this foreword without acknowledging the patience of my wife, Barbara. She has been understanding and tolerant as I spent long hours on these memoirs. I have also appreciated her feed back as she read the chapters in draft form.

And to my children, for whom I have written this, I hope that perhaps you will find some useful lessons. Maybe you will understand the busy life I have led and know that, despite my absences, I have loved you very much.

ACKNOWLEDGEMENT

Like many people, I have been at the task of writing my memoirs for a number of years. It was an ongoing process with no end in sight. Then I met Wade Keller, a former CPA and College Professor, who was willing to help me put it together. Wade began with the notes I had already compiled and came to my home once a week for a 2-hour taping session. When he returned the following week for another taping session he would bring a transcription of the last session and a draft of a chapter. We continued this process with me editing the drafts that Wade prepared until we had the completed product.

On the following pages are frequent references to Swagelok, Nupro, Whitey, Cajon and Goop which are all registered trademarks of Swagelok Company.

Figure 1   In my home office in Naples with Wade Keller.

1

If you quit the rat race, the RATS win!

The Early Years - Laying the Foundation

Looking back I have to say I have had a charmed life. I was born July 8, 1923 in Lima, Ohio, a town of about 40,000 and the county seat of Allen County. It was my good fortune to have the most wonderful of parents, three sisters, two brothers and an extended family of uncles and aunts. Babies were generally not born in hospitals back in the 1920's. I was the second of the six children and seven years old when the last child, my sister Betty, was born. I remember uncle John took Jay, Pat, Tom and myself to the movies while Grandma Falk took care of two-year old brother John. When we returned home dad told us that the stork had come and we had a new sister.

I was named after my father, Francis Joseph Callahan. He was called Frank and I became Joe to distinguish us. My father was born March 27, 1889 in Lima and lived his

75 years there except for his time in the Army in World War I. My father's grandparents were all born in Ireland. His paternal grandparents were Thomas O'Callaghan (born in Ballybunion, Ireland 1810 to 1887) and Mary Hunt (born in Athea, Ireland 1810 to 1877). They were married in 1830 and came to Lima, Ohio in 1863. His maternal grandparents were Patrick O'Keefe (1820 to 1904) and Henora O'Connell (1821 to January 7, 1901). They were married in 1842 and came to Lima in 1860. My father's parents were John Thomas Callahan (born in Ballybunion, Ireland 1850 to September 21, 1899) and Mary Jane Keefe (1850 to November 2, 1902).

Figure 2   My grandfather, John Thomas Callahan about 1897.

My mother, Englebertha Falk, was born November 20, 1893 in Newport, Kentucky. The Falk family arrived from Austria, probably Vienna, in about 1860. My maternal grandfather, Maxmillan Falk, was born in Fond du Lac, Wisconsin in 1869. His parents were Englebert Falk and Mary Oppenaugh. My maternal grandmother, Elizabeth Frye, was born in Newport, Kentucky in 1872. Her parents were Frederick Frye and Catherine Histerman.

My father graduated from high school, which was unusual at that time. Only about 5% of the population back then finished high school. That was probably the equivalent of a college degree today. At age 17 he started working part time as the office boy at Buckeye Pipeline Company. Standing six feet tall he was an exceptional athlete, excelling at baseball and basketball.

On September 5, 1917 he volunteered for the Army. Because of his athletic ability, high school degree and the organizational skills he had learned from working at Buckeye Pipeline he rose quickly through the ranks. He was a leader from the start, promoted to First Sergeant on October 20, 1917. Early in combat he was promoted to Second Lieutenant and later to First Lieutenant.

During boot camp they were in rigorous training. At one point they were making a simulated attack through a barbed wire obstacle course. He led the attack and was the first to step on top of the strands of barbed wire, pushing it down. Immediately on each side the wave of attackers also pushed down on the barbed wire which catapulted my father up in the air. He came down hard and broke his arm. At first the doctors were concerned that he would not make a full recovery. But the fracture did heal and he embarked for Europe on June 12, 1918, engaging in combat the last five months of the war.

Figure 3   My father, Lt. Frank Callahan in WW I.

I have read about what it was like for the American Expeditionary Force in the Great War. Apparently we just sent masses of manpower over, often poorly trained, and the casualties were just horrendous. As a result my father made up his mind at that time that if he had any children, they would all become proficient with a rifle. He also started planting the idea of me going to West Point as soon as he noticed my good grades in school.

As a veteran my father was active in the American Legion. He was Commander of the local Wm. Paul Gallagher Post 96 and was also District Commander. On special occasions they would get dressed up in their uniforms and march in parades with the Drum and Bugle Corps playing. A friend of his, Bill Daley, was a Colonel in the National Guard. We would go up to Camp Perry near Toledo with the guard unit and I would sleep in the tent a few nights with my father. So I was exposed to the military at an early age.

In fact this early involvement with the National Guard probably led me later in High School to be involved with the Civilian Military Training Corps (CMTC). It was one month each summer after my Sophomore and Junior years. The training took place at Fort Benjamin Harrison near Indianapolis. We would practice close order drill, shooting at the rifle range and hand to hand combat with bayonets. We also experienced tear gas drills and KP. My second year I was placed in charge of the tent of eight men. They were mostly older than I was but willing to take orders. It was an early learning experience for me in leadership.

After the war my father went back to work for the Buckeye Pipeline Company. He was the company Secretary and a member of the Board of Directors. His duties included payroll and being sure the company was in compliance with all applicable rules and regulations. He was really the right hand man to the Vice President in charge of the Lima office. Since Lima was the largest pipeline center in the world this was one of the larger offices of the company. He was offered a major promotion when the company moved its headquarters from Lima to New York City on January 1, 1943. The catch was that he would have to move to New York City. But this would have uprooted the family. So he passed up the promotion. Dad became involved in politics, serving two terms as councilman of the 2ⁿᵈ Ward and also presided six months as President of the Council. When he finally retired after about 50 years with the company he was placed in charge of the Lima City Utilities. He served as Director of Public Utilities under both Democrat and Republican Mayors.

Dad also played semi-pro baseball and basketball. At that time, without television and radio, everyone went to the baseball and basketball games. In basketball he played with the Lima White Stars. The White Stars played the outstanding professional teams of those days including the World Champion Buffalo Germans, New York Celts, Oswego Giants, Chicago Hull House Midgets, Toledo Paints and the Ft. Wayne Friars. He became manager in association with Bernie Halloran of the Lima Baseball Club. As a baseball manager one of his players was Joey Brown, the movie star. Joey was the playboy on the team and would always be doing flip-flops and stuff before catching the ball. I remember once at an exhibition game in about 1930, father took me to home plate where I meet Lou Gehrig and Babe Ruth. They each autographed a baseball for me. Unfortunately, I did not appreciate how valuable those signatures would become. And because we didn't have extra baseballs we used them in our baseball games. They were both soon lost.

While in high school I would often be told by admiring fans of my dad, "You'll never be as good as your dad." I took it as a challenge. It probably forced me to play a little better than if I hadn't had that push.

My dad was a local sports personality in the days before television or radio. Theatrical plays were also a big draw. The director would find a well-known local personality to do a dead pan performance amidst the accomplished actors and actresses. It always got a great reaction from the audience when they spotted my father among the actors, carrying a tray as a waiter or some other usually silent routine.

That's how my parents met. My mother was an outstanding singer, a soprano, and performed in plays professionally. They were married on June 29, 1920 in Lima, Ohio at Saint John's Church.

I remember many times as a child being awakened late at night as my parents returned from trips where my mother had competed in singing contests. There would be about six people in the party and they would be happy and boisterous because mother had won first place again. Sometimes she would sing with two other women in a trio. And she also taught piano. Because of her love of music all of us kids learned to play a musical instrument. I played the trombone in the school orchestra. My older sister, Jay (Mary Jane), played the violin. The school was too small for a band. But on one occasion I did get to play in a band. It was for the national American Legion Convention in Cleveland. Our local American Legion formed a band from all the schools in town. About 140 of us from Lima participated and it was the biggest band in the parade.

My parents always liked to travel. We would go in the car. In those days many of the homes would have signs out that they had rooms available for rent. So we would usually rent a room in a family's home along the way. On one trip we went to Yellowstone National Park in Wyoming and to the Badlands in North Dakota. On several trips my mother stayed home with the younger kids. It was probably a vacation for her to send us off for a week or two. On one of those trips we went to Fort Collins, Colorado and visited my Uncle Harry Falk. They had five kids the same ages as our crew, so we had a good time. On another trip without Mom we went to the Battlefield at Gettysburg.

One of the hazards of traveling in a large family was occasionally leaving someone behind after a stop. Once on a trip to Saint Mary's, Ohio for the Peony Festival, we were half way home before someone asked, "Where's John?" We went back and found John, crying after being by himself for almost an hour. We had four or five such mishaps. Kiddie locks on car doors have been a great innovation. On one occasion we were going across the town square and Pat fell out the back door in fairly heavy traffic. Luckily she was not hurt although she and the rest of us were scared half to death.

Figure 4   Our home at 419 McKibben Street. Facing the house, to the right was a large field of grass that I would mow. Behind that field and adjacent to the RR tracks was a larger field on which we played football and baseball. Behind the house I had a basketball board and hoop. Coming out of the house I would turn right to go less than two blocks to church and school.

As a young boy I remember the depression quite well. We lived about a block from where the main line of the Pennsylvania Railroad came through. At that time there were a lot of hobos traveling on the trains looking for work. It really made an impression on me as a kid that men who wanted to work simply couldn't because there were no jobs to be had. These were decent men and you did not need to worry about theft or violence. They had a system of marking homes where a hand out could be expected. Evidently our home was marked because almost every day in the depression hobos would stop by and my mom would always feed them.

As I was growing up we lived in the same house at 419 West McKibben Street. It was a block and a half from St. Rose School where we all attended kindergarten through 12th grade. Classes were taught by Nuns from the Sisters of Charity from Cincinnati, Ohio. The school and church were at the intersection of McKibben Street and West Street. Across from the church on McKibben was the priest's house. Across from the main entrance of the church on West Street was the home where my father had grown up. It continued to be the home of his brothers and sisters. When I was very young I remember they still had gas light fixtures.

There were lots of children in the neighborhood, so we always had plenty of playmates. The Quinn family, two doors to the east of us, had Jim, John, Charlie and Marjorie. Charlie was my age, Jim and John a couple of years older and Marjorie the youngest. Across the street were my classmate, John Riley, and his younger brother, Jim. Around the corner on McDonald Street was the Pellegrinni family. Bob Pellegrinni was in my class. He also had an older brother and two older sisters. The Blust family was about half a block west of us. They had six children including

Ralph who played trombone with me in the school orchestra. Next door to the east of us were the three girls of the Shafer family. There were probably about 15 more kids about my age within a one-block radius of our home.

My Grandfather Callahan had died in 1899 when my father was about 10 years old. Grandmother Callahan, also died a few years after that in 1902. There were ten children: Julius, John, Mike, Cornelius, Josephine, Anna, Mary, Ruth, Leo and my father, Frank. A few of the older ones had already left town. John was in the seminary. But they all returned home and helped raise the younger kids when their parents died. The four youngest were under 12 years of age. At that time there was no social security and extended families took care of themselves.

Of that group of ten children my father was the only one to have children. So along with my two brothers and three sisters, I had an abundance of attentive uncles and aunts. We were the apples of their eyes. It was a routine on Sunday morning after church to go to the Callahan house. They would feed us breakfast and read us the comics. No doubt a welcome break for our parents and one of the few occasions we got bacon and eggs for breakfast.

I was particularly close to Uncle John. He would take me fishing with him three or four times each summer. We would go to Sugar Creek and some other little streams around town. We caught sunfish, catfish and large carp.

In April 1927 my father was coming back from the opening baseball game in Cincinnati and had an automobile accident. His kneecap was shattered and the doctor said he would probably be on crutches the rest of his life. To exercise his knee, every night he would have me, age four, straddle his calf just above the ankle and he would extend his leg lifting me up. After about three years he was able to walk without the crutches and finally got to where he only had a slight limp. During this time with my dad I became fascinated with the crystal radio set on his desk. He would let me listen to it for a little while at night as an inducement to go to bed.

In about 1936 my father was appointed President of the Ohio State Boxing and Wrestling Association. It was his responsibility to be the final arbiter at events when there was a dispute among the referees. I enjoyed going with him to all the Professional Wrestling matches and the Annual Golden Gloves Boxing matches.

My two brothers and I played baseball, basketball and football. But only on one occasion was there a broken bone. In our back yard we had a swing set, teeter-totter and a chain ladder supported by a frame made of two-inch pipe. One day Tom and I were swinging on the swing set. There was a clothesline in front of the swing set. We decided it would be fun to swing as high as we could, jump off and fly over the clothesline. We were having fun when my mother saw us and told us to stop. We kept on. So Mom got angry and said, "GET IN THE HOUSE!!" So in the house we started playing a safe game of cowboys and Indians. Tom was on the arm of a chair, riding it like a horse. I "shot" at him and he fell off and broke his arm in two places.

Another time Tom and I were having a snowball fight. Occasionally one of my snowballs would land on our next door neighbor's porch. The neighbor, Mrs. Diamond, called the police. I had my arm cocked back ready to let loose with another snowball when someone grabbed my wrist. I looked up at a big policeman, well over six feet tall and with an ugly purple birthmark on his face. Holding my wrist with snowball in hand he said, "Are you throwing snowballs?" I brilliantly answered, "No.".

Grandfather Callahan had come from Ireland with his parents in 1865. They came to Lima because it was a railroad town and my Grandfather became a train engineer. My Great Grandfather had married a Hunt and my Grandfather had married an O'Keefe. We were also related to the Duggans, O'Connels, Kings and Moriaritys. As I was growing up my father would often introduce me to someone, saying, "This is your cousin."

Normally you might think of the Irish as being fun loving with a tendency to celebrate with a few drinks. But none of my Irish relatives drank a drop. However my mother's side of the family, the Falks, they were the wild ones. Grandfather Maxmillan Falk, as noted earlier, was born in Fond du Lac, Wisconsin. He moved to Newport, Kentucky where he married Elizabeth Frye in 1890. They had four children in Newport then moved to Lima in 1902 and had five more children.

The Falks were the musical side of the family. Maxmillan led the choir at St. John's Church. And then, on retiring, was succeeded by his son.

Growing up we would drive down to Newport, which is right across the river from Cincinnati, and it would seem like everyone we met was a cousin or great aunt. Both my Falk and Frye Grandparents obviously had a lot of relatives there.

The Falks reunion was always a wild event. When I was 12 or 13 they all came to the home of my Grandparents, Maxmillan and Elizabeth Falk, at 123 Circular Street in South Lima. After a few beers they got their musical instruments out of the attic and started marching up and down the street, stopping traffic with their German band.

Across the street from the Falk home on Circular Street lived two friends, Tom and Jim Lynch. Tom was class of 1964 at the Naval Academy, played varsity football and in 1991 became Superintendent of the USNA. He and I tried to talk his brother Jim into going to Navy. Jim went to Notre Dame instead and excelled at football. He was All-American in college and later played quite a few years in Kansas City in the NFL.

The Falk home was a large house. About 30 years after Grandpa Falk died, my grandmother divided the house into a duplex so she could have some rental income. I remember, shortly after the finish of construction, Uncle Ambie and Uncle Augie decided that they would "bless" the side of the house that was going to provide income. So they got two buckets, one with burning newspapers and the other with water. They ran through the house singing Tantum Ergo, blessing the house with the incense of burning newspapers and spraying "holy" water from the bucket. It was quite a scene with my 80 year old Grandmother chasing them. Perhaps the house was blessed. My Grandmother Falk lived to be 93.

At my mother's 80th birthday party we were in a large hall rented for about 100 people. Her two younger sisters, aunt Mary and aunt Martha made a scene by pounding their fists on the bar and demanding a drink.

When Mary and I were visiting Germany we went to one of the beer halls. Girls were dancing on the tables and the men were lifting up the tables. My wife said, "You are in your element." But it was the Falk side of the family, not my father's Irish side.

The strong family bonds were an essential element in laying the early foundation. Also I received an excellent education at St. Rose School. It began with my sister, Mary Jane, who we called Jay. Jay was two years older than I was. We played together and, after she started kindergarten, our playing consisted of her teaching me what she had learned. Consequently I was the genius of kindergarten and first grade because I had already done all the work. That early start program made it possible for me to get almost all A's through grade school and high school at Lima St. Rose.

Despite my good grades I was thrown out of school one day in the sixth grade. We were starting to learn decimals. This particular nun teacher was not very sharp in math. She made the statement that you could only have two places in a decimal, i.e. 0.24, 0.68 etc. I raised my hand and said this couldn't be right because batting averages had three places such as .333, .278, etc. She got angry and insisted you could only have two places. She was so angry that I kept my mouth shut at the time. The next day at recess I approached Sister Frances Anna who taught math and science in high school and asked her if you could have three places in a decimal. She of course told me you could have three and many more.

After recess, now that I was sure, I raised my hand and informed the sixth grade teacher she was wrong. She got furious and called me up to the front of the room, took out her yardstick and whacked me across the calves of my legs. The yardstick broke and I broke out laughing. She didn't know that I was wearing high top boots under my long pants and the punishment had not hurt at all. She got doubly furious at my laughing and sent me home from school with instructions that I could not come back until my mother came with me. When my mom brought me back the nun told her I had broken her yardstick. I managed to keep my mouth shut and was accepted back in class.

St. Rose was a small school, only about 35 in my graduating class. But we always had a basketball team that could compete with the larger schools. We were started into basketball competition by class in the fourth grade, with encouragement from the older kids looking for fresh talent. Occasionally the fourth grade could beat the fifth grade, but never the sixth, seventh or eighth to win the grade school championship. This early competitive start resulted in above average play in high school.

Basketball was my favorite sport. I started in the fourth grade and played all the way through. I played on the Freshman team and was on the varsity team the last three years. I played forward and backup center and my senior year I was team captain.

Our coach, Tommy Hannon, liked it if you were a little bit of a showman. When I was a junior he was teaching us various tricks. It was normal to only have one referee. After each basket was scored we would jump center the ball. The referee would toss the ball up in the center of the court and the two opposing centers jump for the ball. If the referee's back were to us we would pull on the shorts of our opposing player when the ball was tossed. They would be distracted and turn one way and we would go the other way and get open. Of course their coach would be screaming his head off, but with only one referee they couldn't do anything about it.

Playing forward the coach encouraged me to take a shot right off, hoping to make it and loosen up the defense.

Another mind game we played on the opposing team involved a shot that I practiced making without looking at the basket. It was convenient to practice because the gym was only a couple of blocks from our house. From a certain spot on the court, to the side and a little further out from the foul shot line I practiced making the shot without looking. I could do it at least 50% of the time. So in a game if I were not guarded too close I would look at an opposing player and make the shot.

Two particular games stand out in my memory. My senior year we were playing against our archrival, Lima Saint John's. This was our last game on our home court and I was team captain. As the final seconds ticked down we were behind by one point, 25 to 26. I made a drive to the basket and made it. We won 27 to 26. The team and crowd went wild. I was hoisted up on their shoulders and carried into the locker room.

The other game was when I was named to the All Opponent Team of Dayton Chaminade. We played in Dayton. It was one of those games where I could do no wrong. If I shot the ball it went in. I scored about 16 points which was high score for the game. At one point I was falling down and tried to throw the ball to a teammate. It accidentally went in the basket.

While basketball was my main sport, I also played baseball and football. I was an outfielder and first baseman on the baseball team. I was a pretty good hitter but not an exceptional fielder. When I got a hit it was usually a line drive, hit dead center right at the pitcher. When I came up to bat my teammates would holler at their pitcher, "Be careful because this guy hits it right at you." This style carried over in later years when I started playing golf. I was never one to drive the ball 250 yards. I went more for controlled shots, shorter distances but more accurate. That way I became a pretty good golfer with six hole-in-ones. So far.

Our school did not have a football team as such. Some of us Juniors and Seniors and maybe a few guys from the 9th and 10th grades would play. So we put together an impromptu team. Anyone willing to go out and get pushed around could play. I played end.

We didn't have a football field at our school so we practiced at Northside, a playground that was big enough. George Quatman, head of the Telephone Company bought uniforms for us. We really did not make a very good football team, even when we combined with other Catholic Schools and created Lima Central Catholic. We scheduled to play different schools within a 60 or 70 mile radius.

On one occasion we went down to Springfield with only 25 players, first and second string. I got off the bus and one of the opposing players asked me where the rest of our team was. Of course that was it. Springfield ran out six teams before their first string came out. Their coach was the only real good coach I saw in high school. He took one look at our team and proceeded to replace his players every time during the game he was allowed to make a change. If they had the ball on the right side of the field he would have an end run all the way across to the left side of the field. The first half we were ahead 7 to 6. But the second half they scored about 30 points. I was so tired of running after them in the first half I couldn't run any longer.

I caught about six touchdown passes that year. The coach said I would make All Ohio in college if I played. He would tell the quarterback, "If you can't do anything else, you can always throw it to Joe." Being a basketball player I knew how to fake and dodge.

On one play I was supposed to be the decoy. It was a night game down in Marion, Ohio. I was suppose to pull the defense off and the quarterback would throw the ball to the other end. So I was running down the field not paying much attention. Suddenly I hear people hollering, "Joe, Joe." I was open and when I looked around the ball was about three feet from me. Somehow I caught it and scored a touchdown.

Some of my high school classmates that I spent a lot of time with were Sandy King, Bob Pellegrinni, John Riley, Louie Pentenberg, Jack Walsh, John Dornick and Frank Kuntz. Sandy King was my cousin. In the WW II he drove a jeep for Ernie Pyle in France and later taught History at the University of Dayton. Louie, Jack, John (Riley and Dornick) and I played football on the school team. Louie was also the Center on the basketball team.

Sandy King, Bob Pellegrinni, John Riley and I would ride our bikes to call on some of the girls in our class. I guess we felt there was safety in numbers. Some of the girls that come to mind were Carol Ann Flick, Muriel Mulcahy and Margie Durbin.

A part time job gave me the name "Kate's Boy". Kate had the neighborhood grocery store, which was across the street from our house. At lunch and also after school I would deliver groceries on my bike for Kate to homes in about an eight-block radius. Also I helped John Quinn with his paper route. I had the route memorized and could fill in any time.

Sometimes in the evening a group of us would walk down

town and get a hamburger at the Kewpie or another sandwich shop on Elizabeth Street. Around the corner was a pool parlor and we would slip in for a few games of pool. Word got back to my dad and one night he said, "Son, I don't think it's a good idea for you to be playing pool." I nodded. The next time I was at the pool parlor a wizened old gray haired man was racking the balls for us. He looked up from the rack and said, "Are you Frank Callahan's boy?" I admitted that I was and he said, "Your dad was the best damn pool player this town ever saw." After I reported this to my dad he never said anything else about me playing pool.

I was very fortunate to be able to go to a good Catholic School. It was very strict. The Nuns got you to learn things you needed to know by hook or crook. Singing was a big part of the curriculum. Starting in kindergarten everyone participated in Glee Club. We weren't all that good but it did keep us busy.

I was particularly lucky to have Sister Frances Anna as a Math and Science teacher in high school. She was an excellent teacher of Algebra, Trigonometry, Solid Geometry, Mechanical Drawing, Chemistry and Physics. In addition I had four years of Latin, four years of English and two years of French and History.

I have very fond memories of my 13 years, K-12, at Lima St. Rose. The summer before my senior year I attended Boys' State in Columbus, Ohio. When school resumed I was selected as Senior Class President. I always walked to school. It was only a block and a half. Frequently at lunch - when I wasn't delivering groceries - we would get up a game of bridge with Mom and my two sisters, Jay and Pat. It was Auction Bridge at that time. Later Contract Bridge became popular and we shifted to it. This early training came in handy later at the Naval

Academy when we would play for a penny a point.

After high school I took advantage of a basketball scholarship to go to University of Dayton. This was the Fall of 1941. I played freshman football and basketball. My roommate was Joe Bange. During football season I had a very bad concussion from playing without a helmet. I was running open field against the varsity defensive backfield and got clobbered. For about a month my roommate had to tell me every day what day it was. I missed the whole second half of the season. In basketball I played forward and filled in as guard and center. We had a strong team with five All State players. There were two from Dayton, Ohio, two from Kentucky and one from St. Louis, Missouri. We had ten team members and I was number six, designated the official messenger and frequently filled in at forward, guard or

Figure 5   Front row L-R: Pat, Mom, Jay & Betty. I am behind Pat & Mom. Tom is behind Jay & Betty.

center.

My best friend while at Dayton was Andy Favret who was from Cincinnati. We discovered that our fathers were also close friends. Andy, Joe Bange and I were all in ROTC and majoring in Engineering. In ROTC Andy and I were in the Sterling Rifles which was a special drill squad doing fancy rifle handling and snappy drills. Academics were easy for Andy and myself. One night during study hours a Brother caught us playing pool. He immediately asked, "What are your grades?" We both responded, "All A's" and were told to continue with the pool game.

While in high school during my junior and senior years I had taken exams for my Congressman and Senators to apply for an appointment to West Point which my Dad had encouraged me to do. While at University of Dayton, I received notification that I had received a third alternate position for an appointment to the Naval Academy. That meant that the principal and first and second alternates would have to fail the entrance requirements or the physical for me to get in. I had the registrar's office send in my grades but I did not have high hopes of getting into USNA as a third alternate.

While in high school I had also applied to the Coast Guard Academy in New London, Connecticut. I took national competitive exams to qualify for one of the 200 appointments to the Coast Guard Academy. I was surprised to learn in the Spring of 1942 that I had been accepted at the Coast Guard Academy provided I could pass the physical exam. My brother Tom and I drove up to Cleveland in June and I took the physical for the USCGA. I passed the physical and received orders to report to the Coast Guard Academy on the 14th of July 1942.

While waiting for the 14th of July, my father came home in early July with some exciting news. He said that someone at the bank had told him that the principal and the first and second alternates for my appointment had failed the entrance exams. Therefore I was now in line to be appointed to the Naval Academy.

In a few days I received instructions to report to the Naval Academy to take the entrance physical on July 20th. Since I was already fully accepted at the Coast Guard Academy, my father and I decided that it would be best if I could get a delay for reporting to the Coast Guard Academy to make sure I passed the physical to Annapolis. Frank Knox, Secretary of the Navy, sent me a telegram granting a delay in reporting to USCGA until July 21.

It was fortunate that I didn't just assume I would pass the physical for the Naval Academy for as it turned out the eye refraction test showed I was far-sighted and outside the acceptance range. The doctor told me that the Board would have to meet to decide if I should be accepted. He said to come back tomorrow which was the day I was to report to New London for the Coast Guard Academy.

Being all of 19 years old I responded to the doctor that I required an answer before I left the building that day. I tempered my response by explaining my deadline the following day to report to New London. One thing that attracted me to the Coast Guard was that it was a much smaller school with only about 350 midshipmen. I would have a much better chance to play football, basketball and baseball there, than at the Naval Academy with its 4,000 midshipmen.

It turned out that the Navy made an unusually

expeditious decision and accepted me. I reported to the Naval Academy on July 22, 1942. As I write this at age 75 I am still reading without the help of glasses. And I don't have any trouble following a golf ball several hundred yards either. So I guess my eyes have been all right.

As I mentioned earlier, I was fortunate to be born two years after my sister Jay because she taught me everything she was learning in kindergarten and first grade. Jay was born August 16, 1921. She was a straight A student, played the piano and violin, was on the debate team and was affectionately known as the shortest member of the family. She was about 5 feet 2 inches. My other two sisters were about 5' 10" and all three boys were about 6'. One time we were all at home and Pat looked down at Jay and said, "How did a squirt like you get in this family?"

Jay and I got along very well because we were both academically strong. She and I both tended to be aggressive and take leadership roles. In the summers during High School she became a counselor at a camp that she had gone to in Toledo. She graduated from a Catholic Girl's college in Cincinnati. A few years later while I was at the Naval Academy, Jay went to Georgetown University earning a degree in nursing and a Masters in Psychology. I arranged a blind date for her with my roommate, Edwin A. Burns, and they ended up getting married on April 3, 1948. They made their home in California and raised seven children, all rather bright. These are David (1948), Stephen (1949), Mary Elizabeth (1952), Jeffrey (1954), Daniel (1958), Anna (1960) and Patricia (1961).

My beloved sister Jay died in 1981 at age 60 of Leukemia.

Next after me was my sister, Patricia Ann Callahan, born

Figure 6   Dad and Mom, on Chesapeake Bay at the Naval Academy - June 1945 at my graduation.

December 28, 1924. The thing I remember about Pat is that she was always considered a beauty. She entered beauty contests in the area and would do pretty well. She tried college at St. Mary's in Columbus for a few years but was not really motivated. On September 21, 1946 she married Ed Steiner, a farmer in Kenton, Ohio. They had two girls and a boy. These are Carol Louise (1948), Barbara Ann (1950) and Edwin Louis, Jr. (1952).

One day in 1994 Pat was not feeling well. She went to the doctor and died there in the doctor's office of a heart attack. Their son Eddie is now running the family farm. He and his wife, Kay, have two children.

Next in line is my brother Thomas Bernard Callahan, born December 23, 1926. At age two Tom had blond, curly hair and was a good looking kid. Just after World War II he entered the Army and spent some time in the Philippines.

Figure 7   With Mom and Mary, June 1945.

Figure 8   My father at age 74.

Like our sister Pat, Tom was not highly motivated in college. He did attend some but was more interested in trying a variety of business ventures with varying degrees of success. Tom's first marriage was to Lois Lee Kissel, second marriage to Susan Stant and third marriage to Judy Norton. He has had seven children. The first four were with Lois. They are Jane Marie (1948), Catherine Lee (1949), Thomas Michael (1952), and David Edward (1955). The last three children with Susan are Stephen Matthew (1962), Kelly Katherine (1967) and Terry Louise (1969).

My youngest brother, John Robert Callahan, was born March 21, 1929. John was a great football player. He went to the University of Dayton where he played first string fullback and was team Captain his senior year. He was in ROTC while at the University and received a commission in the Army after graduating. He was sent to Indian Gap, Pennsylvania. The General, learning of John's football ability, wanted to use him on the Indian Gap team. That deferred his having to go to Korea for about a year. He played on the Indian Gap team against the Quantico Marines and other teams in the area. But eventually he did go to Korea as an Army officer. He was a platoon leader in Korea and arrived at the 38th parallel just after the retreat from North Korea ended.

After the war John was drafted by the Washington Redskins to play professional football but decided on a business career instead. He eventually took a distributorship with my company, Swagelok, and was very successful. John has the kind of personality that wears well on customers. He is always friendly and nice to everyone he meets in a very pleasant way.

John married Adele Wise on June 11, 1955 and they had five children. These are Susan Marie (1955), Kevin Francis (1956), Shaun Michael (1958), Colleen Ann (1962) and Mary Cathal (1964). Adele is a registered nurse who still lives in Atlanta, Georgia. John has been married to Patricia Ann (Pat) Simpson since 1992.

My youngest sister, and the last of the kids, was Bertha Elizabeth Callahan, born February 20, 1931 and known as Betty. Betty was always an outstanding student, straight A's like Jay and myself. She was also very talented in music, playing the piano and singing with a beautiful strong voice. She married Tom Williams who was Captain of the basketball team at Ohio State. Naturally Tom and Betty wanted a son to carry on the athletics of his father. They had five girls before having a son! These are Beverly Jean (June 9, 1953), Barbara Joan (January 20, 1955), Deborah Kay (February 1, 1957), Donna Marie (January 4, 1960), Janet Rose (December 11, 1962) and Ronald Lee (May 6, 1964). Their son, Ron, did make a pretty good basketball player. One of their daughters, Beverly, was a good friend of my daughter, Connie.

Tom's family had a fruit distributorship business that he and Betty were very active in. They sold canned goods and also had a fresh produce line. Betty was the company Secretary and in charge of all the accounting.

Betty died at age 60. Like Jay she died of Leukemia.

My parents had six children, three boys and three girls. It is most unusual that all three boys are still living and all three girls have deceased.

Frank and Bertha Callahan lived out their lives in Lima, Ohio. I didn't visit them much after leaving home in 1942. The Navy and a young family kept me busy. When I moved to Cleveland at the end of 1958 I had the opportunity to be with them several times a year.

Dad retired from The Buckeye Pipe Line Company on August 1, 1956 after 50 years of continuous service.

Dad continued to be interested in all sports. He especially enjoyed watching football and baseball on TV. He would always note who the sponsors were of the sports games on TV so he could buy their products. It was his way of thanking the companies for providing the TV coverage. Mom always stayed up to date on all the grandchildren.

In 1962 my father was diagnosed with leukemia. Radiation therapy seemed to keep it under control. In early 1964 they made a trip to Europe. On August 12, 1964 dad left the house around noon to walk to the bank to deposit some checks. He felt dizzy and walked back to the house. Mom drove him to the hospital. I was playing golf at the Chagrin Valley Country Club when I got the call that he was in the hospital. Dad had suffered a ruptured aneurysm of the aorta. Mary and I left within the hour. We arrived at the hospital four hours later. He was already gone.

After dad died, Mom moved from 419 W. McKibben Street to the Westside near Saint Charles Church. A classmate of mine from the Naval Academy, Jack Jennings lived just a couple of blocks away. Jack was a good friend of mine and my parents. I had been best man at his wedding in New London.

Mom did not lack for activities. Of the six children, four of us and our families did not live near Lima after we were married. Mary Jane was married to my roommate, Ed Burns, an officer in the Marine Corps. They spent time in Guam, Washington DC, Boston Massachusetts and California. So they were gone except for the time Ed was in Korea and Mary Jane lived in Lima. Tom lived in Indianapolis and Tucson. John lived in Cleveland and Atlanta. I was in the Navy and spent time on the East and West Coast. However two of my sisters were close by. Betty Williams lived in Lima and Pat Steiner lived on the farm in Kenton about 30 miles from Lima. Betty and Pat's children were 10 of the 32 grandchildren. In addition my mother's sisters, Mary and

Martha had four children who lived in Lima. Mom's brothers, Amby and Max, had about nine children also in Lima.

So after Dad died, Mom had a busy time keeping up with her grandchildren and nieces and nephews. She came to Joe's wedding in Kansas City and to Cleveland for Connie's wedding. In all she kept very busy.

My mother died in September 1978 of cancer of the liver.

Both my Mother and Father were mentally alert and physically active when they died. They deserved to go quickly because they had always lived such fine responsible lives. They earned a quick and painless death without long sickness to go through. At my father's death the City Council of Lima passed a resolution which said in part,

"Be it resolved by the Council of the City of Lima, Ohio that a grateful community sincerely mourns the passing of Frank J. Callahan at the age of 75 years. That on behalf of its members and the entire city administration, Council hereby acknowledges the debt of The City of Lima to Frank J. Callahan and shares with his wife and family a deep sense of loss and hereby offers to them its sincere condolences."

My father set the example that I tried to follow. I was proud of him and always hoped he was proud of me.

Looking back on my childhood in Lima, Ohio I have to say that it was indeed charmed. The love of a close knit family with doting uncles and aunts, the discipline and encouragement of the Nuns at Lima St. Rose, the character and leadership traits developed in competitive sports, all these prepared me well for the adventures ahead.

2

Winning isn't everything, but losing is nothing. Show me a good loser and I will show you a loser.

Naval Academy

The United States Naval Academy has a proud history going back to its founding in 1845. Through the efforts of Secretary of the Navy George Bancroft, the Naval School was established at a 10 acre Army post named Fort Severn in Annapolis, Maryland on October 10, 1845. The initial class consisted of 50 midshipmen and 7 professors. The curriculum included mathematics and navigation, gunnery and steam, chemistry, English, French and natural philosophy.

Five years later in 1850 the name was changed to United States Naval Academy. The curriculum, then as now, required midshipmen to study four years at the Academy and train aboard ships each summer. As the U.S. Navy grew over the years, the Academy expanded. The campus of 10 acres increased to 338 acres. The student body grew to a brigade size of 4,000. In 1933 Congress authorized the awarding of Bachelor of Science degrees.

I arrived at the Naval Academy for my pre-induction physical on July 20, 1942. The first two nights I stayed with two other applicants at the only hotel in town, Carvell Hall. As I related in the last chapter the physical indicated I was farsighted, outside the acceptable range, but the Navy decided to take me anyway.

Figure 9 Large Sloop used for recreation at the Academy

On reporting in I was assigned to a cutter crew. This was a crew of six that worked together and did a lot of rowing and sailing. Al Whittle, one of the midshipmen in my cutter crew, became a life long friend and a four star admiral. Al was on the K-2 when I was on the K-1 and he later had command of the Sterlet after I had served there. He commanded a nuclear submarine and I worked in the nuclear program. So when we visited in later years we had a lot to talk about. A couple years ago he tied up his boat at my dock at our home in Naples for a month. Sadly Al recently died of lung cancer.

Before we were sworn in we were given the royal treatment. Then after being sworn in, it was no more Mr. Nice Guy. We followed orders, saluted and said "Yes Sir"! Plebe summer was a two-month boot camp before classes started. We did a lot of close order drill, manual of arms, marching to the rifle and pistol range, running on the obstacle course and swimming tests. This was the time we received sailing experience. Six guys would crew on a little knockabout, a 20-foot sloop or on

Figure 10   With Ed Burns, my roommate at the Academy and later, brother-in-law. We are on Beacon Street in Boston when I was attending MIT in February 1948.

Figure 11   Sailing race at Naval Academy.

a ketch. We would also crew on a larger sloop that had a 100-foot mast. After being there two weeks I was assigned to the 20th Company and a room. My roommates the first two years were Ed Burns from Michigan and Dave Munns from Minnesota. Ed was a great sports fan. He knew everything about baseball, basketball and football.

For the last year all of our class in the 20th Company were moved to the 12th Company and Ken Ackley took Dave Munns place as the third roommate with Ed and me.

In September with the start of classes the upper classmen returned and the hazing began in earnest. This was designed to build discipline and weed out the ones that couldn't take the stress. The whole corps always ate at the same time in the big mess hall in Bancroft Hall. Upperclassmen would single us out and ask a question. Normally we would not know the answer. We would then be asked the same question at the next meal and if we still didn't know the answer we would be ordered to "shove out". This meant sitting at the table without a chair. But you had to look like you were sitting in a chair. This was very hard on the legs until you were told to sit down again. The questions concerned all kinds of rules, arcane and otherwise, songs and verses. One of the simpler questions was, "What's up?" The proper answer was "Fidelity, Sir!" because that was at the top of our belt buckles.

Hazing could also occur anytime an upperclassman saw us doing something we shouldn't be doing. This could be things like not having your eyes straight ahead or not walking down the precise center of the hall and making right angle turns. Punishment included being called to the upperclassman's room and told to "knock off your class year" which for us meant doing 46 pushups since we were the class of 1946. We would generally get a broom applied to our posterior as well.

There was some relief from the harassment. Each plebe, or sometimes a room, would be assigned first classmen who would not haze. These were our mentors helping us get through the hazing from everyone else. My roommates and I were assigned R. J. Young and Dave Zachry as our friendly first classmen. We could also get spooned. This meant an upperclassman would seek us out, shake hands with us and thereby indicate he would also be our mentor. Bill Boose, an upperclassman from Lima, Ohio spooned me. I was also spooned by the center on our company basketball team, Shannon Crammer. Shannon was class of '44, ended up in submarines and became an Admiral. Another guy, Bucky Dietzen, a friend of Dave Zachry was a big football player on the Junior Varsity. Bucky would come around giving me a hard time. I would get sassy with him and he would take the broom to me. One night I took the broom away from him and started chasing him down the hall. He got another broom and we had a broom fight. He ended up spooning me and we became good friends. Bucky, like Shannon Crammer, ended up in submarines and made Admiral. In all I had about 15 upperclassmen that spooned me.

The sports activities were very competitive. I had been captain of my high school football team and had lettered in three sports. But that was the norm for the Naval Academy. There were 1250 in my class, over all about 3250, and all in superb physical condition.

My plebe year I played freshman basketball up until February. I was playing in a scrimmage against the varsity. The first half I was top scorer with 8 points and I held the top scorer on the varsity team to only 2 points. We were about three minutes into the second half when I got an open shot near the foul line. I shot it one handed. It went around the rim about three times and then fell off. The freshman coach got all upset. He had already been complaining about me taking one handed shots, which is the way we had been playing at St. Rose and at Dayton. The coach pulled me out of the game and started screaming at me for taking "crazy" shots. So after that I quit and played on the intramural team. All three years our company won the regimental championship.

I also played softball plebe year and we won that regimental championship also. My roommate, Ed Burns, also played on the championship softball team. There was a write up about us in "The Log", the monthly journal of the Naval Academy. The story cited us for batting a 1000. Either Ed or I was batting 550 and the other 450. So as a room we were batting at 1000.

The basketball and softball wins helped 20th Company achieve the Color Company award for the year, which was a distinct honor. The Color Company award was based on our performance on the parade field and athletic programs. The following year our company placed second

Academically I was well prepared by Lima St. Rose and Dayton University. If you had a reputation of being pretty good in the classes you were called a savoir. I was generally a savoir, especially the first year. In the evening there would be classmates coming to my room for a little extra instruction, trying to get prepared for the next day's classes.

The Naval Academy uses self-teaching to a great extent. In all the courses we would be given a certain assignment for each day. Then at the beginning of each class we would be tested on the assignment for that day . After that the professor would answer questions or lecture on the material. Some people would say this was not a very normal way of teaching. But after a while you understood that you could learn anything if you just studied the book. This pedagogy was very effective in preparing for service on board ships. As new technology came on line we would have to learn it and then teach it to the crew. An example was the radar and sonar upgrades on board submarines. As the officer in charge I had to study the manual

Figure 12   Parade Drill in Full Dress.

to learn how to run and repair the new electronic equipment before I could teach it to the crew. Also those of us who went on to graduate schools found that we were well prepared to study the advanced courses. I actually made better grades at MIT (Bachelors and Masters) than I did at the Academy.

The pace at the Academy was always hectic. Before every meal we had meal formation in the proper uniform. We would sometimes have to change uniforms for certain classes. Generally if we were doing something of a seamanship nature we would wear the old white sailor uniform with the bouncy top. Going to classes we would wear the blue serge uniforms with white shirts, French cuffs, cuff links and properly tied ties. Of course we always had proper haircut and shoes brightly shined. There could be no lint on the uniform and all brass glistened.

We always marched in formation to class. Each company would have four units marching off to different classes. The officer of the day would have a midshipman as the orderly taking down names for demerits for such things as not keeping in step or talking in ranks.

Between the last class and formation for the evening meal we had intramural sports activity. After the sports event we had 20 minutes to shower and get dressed for the meal formation. Taking longer than three minutes in the shower was sure to subject you to screams from your roommates.

Once a week we had a retreat where all the companies would march in review with the band playing. It was really awesome. At that time there were 20 companies with about 200 in each company. Everyone would be shined up carrying rifles, swords and flags. Each company was graded on how sharp your ranks were and how precisely the marching orders were executed. This was part of the Color Company competition.

So there were three meal formations each day, plus formations to march to class. It was a challenge to always be in the right uniform, on time and not get demerits.

Figure 13   Color Guard in Rotunda of Bancroft Hall.

On Saturday and Sunday afternoons of Plebe year we would have a few hours that we could go into Annapolis. But since we only received $11 a month from our midshipman pay there was often no reason to go into town. Midshipman pay was about $110 per month. All but $11 was held in our account to purchase uniforms while at the Academy and a fund we would need at graduation to buy ensign insignia, etc. My Mom would send me $15 to $20 a month from her singing income. She knew my Dad would let me get by on what I was paid.

In my company there were four other guys that I would get together with and play bridge. These were Jack McKay, Red Layton, Al Carnegie and J.D. King. With five players we generally had four available for a game. Jack McKay also played varsity basketball. His roommate, Red Layton was from Wooster, Ohio. Back then when I played bridge I could keep up with every card that had been played and which cards were still out. We would play for a penny a point and I would frequently make more playing bridge than my $11 cadet pay. In later years J.D. King became an expert bridge player. There was an article in the Wall Street Journal, left column front page, about J.D. moving around from town to town playing bridge with women so they could get their masters points.

The second and third years we took courses in electricity, thermodynamics and differential calculus. We had to be able to make the calculations for the trajectories when shooting guns at long range. The academy taught about 20 foreign languages. I took French, one of the easier ones. The language savoirs were taking Russian, Japanese and Chinese. We also became acquainted with small ship seamanship by running about in patrol crafts. We had crewed on knockabouts in plebe summer. Now we were able to volunteer to crew on larger sloops. Al Sheppard was one of the sailors who let me crew when he was skipper of one of the larger sloops.

I made two summer cruises while at the academy and became acquainted with the surface navy. In July of 1943 I was on a battleship, the USS New York. We did all the dirty work that a seaman sailor would do. For example holystoning the deck. With blocks of stone that must have looked like old time bibles, we would scrub the wood deck of the ship and then wash it down with seawater. The next year, July 1944, my cruise was on board the USS Arkansas, another battleship. We sailed down to the Caribbean, went ashore in Trinidad and had a beer party. Our guns on ship were 20mm and 40mm anti-aircraft and a battery of 16-inch guns, which would roll the ship when we fired them. At one point a drone plane was sent out for target practice. Apparently it was supposed to be difficult to hit and no one had hit it in a long time. The brass got a little upset when we hit it the first few minutes and didn't have anything to shoot at for the rest of the day.

At the end of that cruise we had a two-week leave. I applied to go to New London, Connecticut to obtain submarine experience during my leave. I was assigned as a midshipman observer on the submarine USS (S 48), which was the last riveted submarine built. All subsequent submarines were built with welded hulls. Riveted boats tended to leak through the rivets. When we got down to 100 feet the drain pump couldn't pump the water out fast enough. So we had to stay less than 100 feet deep. The S48 was the first U.S. boat with a stern torpedo tube. Another feature of the S48 was two six-inch diameter glass portholes in the front of the conning tower. This is the only submarine I was on that you could look out at the deck while submerged and watch fish swimming by.

I was attracted to submarines for several reasons. For one thing, submarines were a very potent weapon for our side in World War II. In the early days the Japanese were knocking out allied surface ships and submarines were the most effective weapon. The US submarine force was the only thing that kept the Japanese from taking Australia.

The other thing that attracted me to submarine service was the contrast with service on a battleship. The large surface ships were to some degree an extension of the academy with its inspections, spit and polish and military order, a lot of screaming to get things done. On submarines you called the men by their first names, you trusted other crew members and

Figure 14   Midshipman Francis Joseph Callahan, Jr. - April, 1944

they trusted you. There was high morale because of the shared danger and close quarters. I always felt my crewmembers who worked for me tried to do everything right because they didn't want me to get in trouble with the Captain. Sometimes the whole crew would be called out with short notice. If you happened to be in your bunk and didn't have time to get dressed you just showed up in you skivvies.

Even though submarines might be loose on military protocol we were extremely tough and disciplined on performance. Because of the immediate danger if you made a mistake, there was zero tolerance. For example on rigging for a dive, if an officer made a mistake he was out of the submarine service. An enlisted man might get one warning and then out on the second mistake.

So for those reasons, in my final year at the academy I applied for submarine duty. Such requests were based on class standing. Based on Academics, Conduct and Leadership I graduated 77 out of a starting class of 1250 with a GPA of 3.39. On June 6, 1945 I was awarded a BS degree from the United States Naval Academy and Commissioned an Ensign in the United States Navy. My orders provided for one month's leave, followed by one month in Air Observer Training at Jacksonville Naval Air Base before reporting to New London, Connecticut for the next Submarine School.

3

The next best thing to brains is silence

Marriage and Family

MARY ELIZABETH KROUSE

My plebe year at the Naval Academy was 1942-43. While home for Christmas I went to a dance at the Memorial Hall. I didn't have a date that night. Just dropped in with a few buddies. I noticed an especially attractive girl and asked her to dance. That's how I met Mary Elizabeth Krouse. Mary and I had a few dates before I returned to Annapolis. Then we started corresponding. During the next summer when I had some leave we continued dating. One thing we really enjoyed was going swimming at Schoonover's private pool east of Lima

Mary was born February 18, 1926 in Cleveland, Ohio. Her parents were Rollo Burdette Krouse (February 22, 1894 to December 27, 1968), a medical doctor, and Theresa F. Lennon (March 29, 1893 to June 5, 1962). Her father's parents were Lorenzo Krouse (born May 22, 1848) and

Figure 15   With my Father, June 1945.

Mary Eliza Garotte (born September 17, 1858). Her mother's parents were Patrick Lennon (born April 25, 1863) and Catherine Mary Toner (born December 15, 1862)

I would kid Mary that she chased me her senior year in high school. She came from Lima to Baltimore, just 30 miles from the Naval Academy, to attend a small Catholic school named Illchester. The school was used primarily to train nuns. Her father was not Catholic, so it may have been that he just thought that would be a safe place for Mary to finish high school. After high school she attended Trinity College in Washington DC which is also a Catholic school. She was able to come to Annapolis on weekends during my First Class (Senior) year. She would come over on the bus with some other girls and we would go to dances, football games, sailing or other special events on the weekends.

A few days before my graduation from the Academy on June 6, 1945, Mary and I became engaged. I had one month of leave before my duty assignment in Jacksonville, Florida.

Figure 16   After the wedding. Bearded man is
Patrick Lennon, Mary's grandfather.

Figure 17   Cutting the Wedding Cake, June 30, 1945.

We went home to Lima with no definite plans on just when to get married. But as we considered that we would be separated for a long period with me in the Navy we decided to go ahead and get married. We were married on June 30th at St. Rose Church in Lima, Ohio. My best man was Andy Favret, a good friend of mine while I was at Dayton University. Andy had just graduated from West Point. Mary's maid of honor was Alice Marie Simons Chermak, her close friend from Lima.

On July 8, 1945 I reported to the Naval Air Station in Jacksonville with my wife of one week. We stayed in a boarding house for my one-month training assignment as an air observer. While there I also completed a survival swimming course to get a AAA certificate, which was required of all the pilots.

Figure 18   Our Wedding day. On our right are Mary's parents, Rollo and Theresa Krouse. On our left are my parents, Frank and Bertha Callahan.

After that assignment we moved to New London, Connecticut where I reported aboard the USS Cuttlefish (SS171) on August 6, 1945 to await the start of submarine school. On VJ Day, August 15th, I was on the Cuttlefish standing duty with the ship's duty officer. Victory celebrations were starting all over because of the Japanese surender. The duty officer said, "I'll stand the duty. Why don't you go into town to be with your wife."

It was a chaotic day. The roads were crowded with cars and I didn't have a car at that time. So it took me about two hours to work my way back into New London and celebrate the end of the war with Mary.

I graduated from sub school on December 22, 1945. We had a one-week leave so we went home to Lima. Mary was two or three months pregnant and had a miscarriage while we were home for the holidays. Her father, Dr. Rollo Krouse, was very concerned and requested that Mary stay in Lima so he could run a complete physical while I returned to New London for a month of Radar and Sonar School. Dr. Krouse found that her blood sugar was very high and determined that she had diabetes. Insulin treatment and other routines were started and Mary returned to New London on about the first of February.

If Mary's blood sugar was not controlled, diabetes could result in kidney failure, blindness and leg amputation because of poor circulation. Also, if pregnancy occurred, the chance of delivering a live baby was only about 1%. We took it very seriously.

At that time the leading research group doing work on diabetes was the Joslin Clinic in Boston. The Joslin Clinic had been established in 1898 and was affiliated with Harvard Medical School. Mary went there shortly after returning from Lima to be trained on how to take care of herself. The clinic specialists taught tight control of blood sugar. Fortunately we came in contact with Dr. Priscilla White at the Joslin Clinic. Dr. White was beginning to run tests and do research to help diabetics have successful pregnancies. Dr. White became a dear friend. Because of her we were able to have a family. Mary's father cautioned us not to have children. But Mary was determined to take the risks.

When Mary became pregnant she was required to have hormone injections daily. These were given in the buttocks with a syringe three inches long and 3/4 inches in diameter. It was quite a volume to be taking daily. Pregnant with Joe III, Mary went in the hospital six months before delivery and had to stay in bed most of the time. As Dr.

White improved her research the hospital stays were shortened. With Connie the hospital stay was three months and with Tim only one month.

All three of our children were born by cesarean section. The problem that a diabetic has giving birth is that the kidneys would start failing and the nitrogen level would rise. It was important to be able to take the baby by cesarean section before the mother suffered kidney damage and the baby died. It was really experimental new medicine. Up until that time hardly any diabetics had children. Dr. White was running about 95% live births.

We tried to keep Mary's blood sugar around 100. If she exercised more one day than another she could have an insulin reaction due to low blood sugar. The reactions could come on quickly. If the reactions came on too quickly and Mary was not able to ingest food to raise her sugar level, she would go into convulsions. The clinic had taught us to tightly control her sugar level and Mary would sometimes control it too tightly. That's when she would get in trouble and have a reaction. About one in fifteen reactions would result in convulsions. This would happen about every three or four months. The only way to come out of the convulsions was to take a 50 to 100 cc of glucose administered intravenously. Her veins were so small I could never learn to give her this injection.

One of the bad reactions occurred just after Tim was born. Mary was taking about 50 units of insulin a day before Tim was born and continued with this same dosage after Tim's birth. Later we found out she only needed 30 units to control her blood sugar. A reaction occurred and I took her to the local hospital in Arlington, Virginia. We were in the emergency room and the doctors refused to give her the glucose on my word. They insisted that they had to have a blood sugar test first, thinking she might be in diabetic coma. So Mary was in convulsions for 45 minutes before they brought her out of it. This was typical of a considerable number of hospital emergency rooms we had to use and was very irritating. It was different in hotel rooms. On our world travels she would occasionally have a bad reaction in a hotel. I could always get a hotel doctor to give her intravenous glucose and it would be over in about 10 minutes. The only place I ran into a doctor that would listen to me was in Acton, Massachusetts. Dr. Borden recognized that I understood what was going on and consequently asked me to speak to the doctors at Concord Hospital.

This nightmare of Mary going into convulsions and me not being able to give intravenous glucose came to an end around 1967. We were fortunate to have Dr. Nancy Johnson when we lived in Chagrin Falls. Dr. Johnson was always willing to make a house call and give an intravenous shot of glucose even though she was very busy delivering half the babies in Solon, Ohio. Nancy introduced us to glucagon made by Eli Lily. With glucagon I could just give Mary a shot and in 15 minutes she would come out of the reaction. It was not necessary to find a vein. Once I got glucagon we never had to go back to an emergency room with insulin shock. Nancy has always been a good friend. She made it possible for us to travel without the worry and problems of insulin reactions.

One example occurred in 1980 when we lived in Daisy Hill. Mary was talking on the telephone with our neighbor, Mary Weber, and started to slur her speech and lose comprehension. An attack was coming on fast. Mary Weber called me at the office and also called another neighbor,

Juanita King. Mary and Juanita rushed over to the house, broke a window to get into the breakfast room. Mary was in full convulsions. I rushed in just then. The neighbors were anxious to call an ambulance but I just gave her a glucagon shot. Ten minutes later Mary looks at me and says, "What are you doing here?" She was perfectly lucid. To our neighbors, Juanita and Mary, it seemed like a miracle.

Another problem that Mary had was osteoporosis. Mary began to have frequent broken bones. The first occurrence was in 1980 when we had planned a trip with Dale and Juanita King. They were going to fly with us out to Denver to play in a Member-Guest tournament at Dale's old course there, the Cherry Hills Country Club. We were getting ready to go to the airport when Mary called from the bathroom that she had fallen. She kept saying that we could still go on the trip but I called an ambulance and took her to Hillcrest Hospital. She had broken her back. As time went on she broke her arm twice, both wrists at different times, her foot, her back again and three ribs. Every time I called the emergency squad to take her in they would question me to determine if I were a wife beater.

That was really a tough period for about ten years. Finally we went to the Cleveland Clinic. They had a new treatment using fluoride salts and hormones in addition to calcium. It was experimental. Mary had to take it every day and the major side effect was being sick to the stomach. The hormones would cause the bones to pick up the fluoride and calcium and thus be strengthened considerably. After she had been on the treatment for about ten months she fell down and was happy because she hadn't broken anything. It was the first time in years that she had fallen and not broken something.

Figure 19   With Mary and son Joe, Christmas 1947.

FRANCIS JOSEPH CALLAHAN III

Our first child was Francis Joseph Callahan III, born December 27, 1946 at the Faulkner Hospital in Boston. At that time I was attached to the USS Grouper (SS214) which was being overhauled at the shipyard in Portsmouth, New Hampshire about 70 miles north of Boston. Mary's mother, Theresa Krouse, came to be with us. She rented part of a two family house in Arlington, Massachusetts. For about two weeks I was back and forth between there and the Grouper. On January 15, 1947 I was assigned to MIT (Massachusetts Institute of Technology) to obtain a degree in Electrical Engineering.

Mrs. Krouse had found an apartment on Beacon Street near MIT, which we rented. The apartment was one big room with a kitchen. A convertible sofa served as living room furniture in the day and our bedroom at night. We put Joe's crib in one corner with a bookcase separating the nursery from the rest of the room. That's where Joe got started.

From the Beacon Street apartment I walked to school. We used the baby buggy to bring groceries home. I was making $210 a month as a JG and the apartment was $100 a month plus utilities. The Navy paid school expenses but we had to cover everything else. Fortunately I had built up some savings while getting pay and a half for submarine duty while on the Grouper. Mary's mother used to send us care packages. Her idea of what we needed was not exactly on target. She would send smoked oysters and stuff for cocktail parties. We barely had enough money to buy bacon and eggs, much less whiskey. We often had some rather exotic food while waiting for payday to show up.

Figure 20   Our home in Chula Vista while on board Volador. Son Joe on the curb.

I finished at MIT in September 1948 with a Bachelors of Science in Electrical Engineering (BSEE). On October 1st I reported for the new construction crew of the USS Volador (SS490) at Portsmouth Naval Shipyard in Maine.

At this time we finally bought our first car, a Mercury Club Coupe that had about 40,000 miles on it. This nearly ended our marriage because I had to teach Mary how to drive a car. Since then I have recommended, when asked, that no husband should ever teach his wife how to drive.

We rented a small red house in Kittery, Maine that was about three blocks from the shipyard. The house had a kerosene hot water heater in the basement. One night when we came home the basement was orange with flames. The candles in the living room had bent over from the heat. This was in the winter. A fire was raging out of control in the kerosene heater. I went down in the basement, found a large piece of red cloth and threw it on top of the water heater to smoother the flames. The red cloth was a couch cover that Mary had sewn. She complained for years of my fire fighting efforts because I ruined her couch cover. About a week later the heater fire was out of control again while I was on duty. Mary was in the house with Joe and couldn't control the fire. She called the fire department and was standing on the porch with Joe when she saw the volunteer firemen running past the house down to the fire station at the end of the road. She hollered, "Help! The fire is in here!" They responded, "Too bad lady. We don't get paid unless we are on the truck." But they did finally get the fire out without the house burning down.

I rode the USS Volador through the Panama Canal to San Diego from January to April 1949. Mary and Joe went to Lima and then met me in San Diego and we rented a house in Chula Vista. On August 26, 1950 I reported aboard the USS Sterlet (SS392) at Mare Island Naval Shipyard. Our mission was to take the Sterlet out of "mothballs" in preparation for duty in the Korean War. Joe was almost four, a cute little red headed kid. We lived in a Quonset hut and in good old Navy tradition, five o'clock was cocktail hour. Every night we had to find little Joe as he wandered around to the various Quonset huts, scavenging peanuts, cheese and crackers and other snacks. Everyone liked him. After about a month the Sterlet moved down to San Diego. This time we got a house in Pacific Beach about one block from the ocean.

On February 19, 1951 I was detached from the Sterlet with orders to report back to New London for assignment to the new construction crew of the USS K-1 (SS K-1). We drove cross country in our Mercury Coupe, stopping in Lima for a few days.

Back in New London, Connecticut we bought our first house. It was at 86 Summer Street and cost $12,500. Joe started kindergarten and first grade at the public school there about a block and a half from our house. At that time Mary became pregnant with our second child. Fortunately New London is not too far from Boston. So she went back and forth to Boston to see Doctor Priscilla White. Connie was born April 7, 1953. We were thankful again to the Joslin Clinic for their research and breakthroughs, which were allowing diabetics to have live births. Joe seemed to accept Connie pretty well and there weren't any problems. In fact Joe always played well with all the kids around.

On June 8, 1953 I reported again to MIT, this time for a Masters in Nuclear Engineering. We rented a place in Arlington, Massachusetts for the year I was in school at MIT. Joe made his first communion there.

After completing the Masters I was assigned to Bureau of Ships, Nuclear Propulsion Division and Naval Reactors Branch, Atomic Energy Commission in Washington, DC on July 22, 1954. For several months my assignment was to

Figure 21 Our home in Acton, Massachusetts, one of three Lottery Houses built in 1772. Looking across the yard you can see Strawberry Lane, where Acton patriots on April 19, 1775 marched to THE bridge for THE fight.

travel around the country and visit various nuclear power plants. Then on September 4, 1954 we bought a home at 2323 Burlington Street, Arlington, Virginia. This was our second home purchase and cost $16,000. Joe attended St. Agnes School and became active in the Cub Scouts. Mary didn't take to that cub-scout-mother stuff. So I ended up taking care of the scouts on Saturdays. Washington DC is a great place for field trips. I would take the scouts to such places as the Smithsonian and the National Planetarium.

Tim was born February 28, 1956 while I was with the Bureau of Ships. Like with Joe and Connie, he was born in Boston under the care of Dr. Priscilla White. The Joslin Clinic procedures for diabetics having successful pregnancies were improving. On this last pregnancy Mary was only in the hospital for one month prior to Tim's birth.

A traumatic event happened on the day Joe completed

the 7th grade. We had moved to 252 Great Road, Acton, Massachusetts in January 1958 when I took the position of Director of Kenmore Research Company in Framingham. We lived in a sparsely populated area with a large open field across from the house. Joe's friend, Murphy, lived about a quarter mile down the road. The first day out of school for the summer Joe and Murphy were building a fort or some such activity. Murphy had hedge clippers and accidentally clipped Joe's ring finger on his left hand. I was out cutting the grass. Joe came screaming home with a cloth around his finger. Mary got all upset, came out the door carrying two year old Timmy and fell down the steps. Tim wasn't hurt even though he was thrown on the ground. I rushed everyone to the doctor's office in Acton. The doctor took care of Mary first while the nurse worked on Joe. I went back and found the severed part of the finger and brought it back to the doctor. They worked a long time before finally deciding the finger could not be reattached. Fortunately the damage to the rest of his hand was repaired and healed completely.

In November, 1958 we moved to 64 Maple Street, Chagrin Falls a suburb of Cleveland where I became President of Nupro Company. Joe and I would frequently go to football and baseball games together. He finished grade school at two different public schools and then went to Gilmour Academy for high school. For sports he tried basketball and cross country but his main sport was soccer. He did very well at Gilmour.

During the summers he liked to spend time with his grandfather Krouse. Dr. Rollo Krouse had retired from his medical practice in Lima to his 5,000 acre ranch in Kansas. Dr. Krouse would take him out to the milo and soybean fields early in the morning with a machete. Joe would use

Figure 22   Joe, standing in front wearing shirt, with gun crew in Vietnam.

the machete to cut cane out of the fields so the crops could be harvested. Dr. Krouse would come back for him at noon so he could get something to eat and then take him back for the afternoon. Joe always enjoyed the out doors. He continued with his Boy Scout activities all the way through high school.

After high school Joe decided to go to Kansas State University and major in Agriculture Economics in preparation for eventually running the Krouse ranch. After a year of college the Vietnam War was heating up and Joe decided to volunteer. He didn't have to go because he had a college deferment. But he went anyway.

In high school he had driven a Volkswagen with a stick shift which I had brought from Massachusetts. So when the army asked if he could drive a stick shift the answer was yes. After basic training he was assigned to drive a truck.

Figure 23   Ginny and our first grandchild, Tricia at about age 2.

Figure 24   From left, Ginny's sister Jodie, Ginny, Joe & Connie.

Figure 25   Tricia and Joseph, February 1988.

Figure 26   Son Joe about 1986.

Figure 27   Tricia at age 15.

From there he went to tank driving and from there he was advanced into artillery. Since he had one year of college he was sent to the sixty day "Instant Sergeant Program" and promoted to Sergeant.

With one year left he was sent to an advanced fire base station in Vietnam. It was a remote area supplied by helicopters. He received two Bronze Stars for Bravery. Later he protested to me that he didn't really deserve the award. The enemy was infiltrating their base station and his 155mm was the only one that kept firing. He said, "If I didn't keep firing they were going to come in and kill us." Of course, I think he deserved the Bronze Stars and am very proud of him.

During the year he only left the fire base station one-day. The gun barrel needed to be rebored after all the firing. He went in with the helicopter to be sure the boring was done right.

Returning from Vietnam Joe finished his degree at Kansas State University where he met his wife, Ginny. They were married on June 23, 1973. Their daughter, Tricia, was born June 8, 1978 and their son Joseph was born May 8, 1981.

Tricia was the first of our grandchildren. She has always been a quiet, serious girl. Growing up on a farm she was very interested in animals. They had every type of farm animal as well as a ferret, guinea pigs, gerbils, a snake and a parakeet. The ferret would run all over the house, the parakeet was trained to land on her shoulder and she fed mice to the ten-foot snake. Tricia has always been a good student. One of the things I admire about her is she has high principles and will not put up with any nonsense from anyone. Her senior year in high school she attended a boarding school. When her roommate was smoking Tricia kicked her out and got a new roommate. For college she decided to go to Creighton, a Jesuit college in Omaha, Nebraska. She started out with the idea of being a veterinarian. I asked her, "Do you want to be a vet for large farm animals like horses and cattle?" She replied that she really didn't like dealing with large animals. So I said, "I suppose you will be working with dogs and cats." To which she replied that, no, she really didn't like treating dogs and cats. Then I said, "Why are you going to be a vet?" That's when she decided to be a medical doctor. But after being in pre-med a while I think she is now majoring in history with plans to be a teacher. Tricia also enjoys the out doors, going fishing, hunting and shooting skeet.

On one occasion Joe and Ginny took a couple of her

friends and horses in the horse trailer to a remote area camping and horseback riding for a couple of weeks. At this point I don't think she has had a real serious boy friend. Her standards are probably too high for most boys. Tricia may not have decided yet what she wants to do with her life. But whatever she decides, it will be very worthwhile.

Figure 28   Joseph about age 8, with his ferret.

Joseph is three years younger than his sister, Tricia, and a good bit different. A dyed in the wool hunter and fisherman, he was on the state skeet championship team when a junior in high school. His interest in animals is more from the standpoint of hunting rather than ranching. Joseph likes to kid his dad and his uncle Tim. They have a good relationship.

When Joseph was about 13 I went on a fishing trip with the family to the famous Whitewater in Arkansas. We were

Figure 29   Joseph shows off his catch.

below a dam in the river. The water would get shallow over night and then in the morning they would open the dam, generating electricity. When the water was deep enough we could go out in boats fishing for trout. Joseph and I were in one boat and Joe, Ginny and Tricia in the other boat. As we started off, Joseph announced to everyone, "Grandpa probably won't catch any fish. He doesn't know how to fish." Joseph and I began fishing. About two minutes after I made my first cast I caught a nice trout. I ended up catching about ten trout to Joseph's chagrin as he didn't catch any. He found out his grandfather had done a little fishing in his life and knew how to set a hook.

Both Tricia and Joseph are kids that have grown up on the farm and developed a good sense of responsibility. I believe they both have pretty high standards on how they intend to live and what they are going to do.

Ginny has been a wonderful wife for Joe. She is very level headed and solid, responsible with the kids and goes with the flow with respect to Joe. Ginny was diagnosed with bone cancer in 1998. It had started as a small cancer on her breast. It is hopefully in full remission. Her attitude has been an inspiration to everyone who knows her. She says, "Before the cancer I didn't know how long I would live. And now I still don't know how long I will live. So what's different?"

Joe and Ginny worked the ranch together while raising their two kids. At times they ran 1600 head of cattle. They had goats, peacocks, hunting dogs and a Limousin bull named Rufus. No one could do anything with Rufus except Ginny. The bull would follow Ginny wherever she wanted it to go. She would walk with her back to it without any fear. Of course they also had a lot of cats. Once they were receiving a delivery of feed supplement. The delivery man was told they had 31 cats. He replied, "That's not near enough." When you have grain in a silo you need a lot of cats to control the rats.

Joe enjoys hunting and is an excellent marksman. He has made a complete study of firearms including the composition of gunpowder and bullets. He shoots prairie dogs at 600 yards by figuring the drop over that distance.

Joe and Ginny make a great couple and have done a wonderful job raising Tricia and Joseph.

Figure 30   With sons Joe and Tim at Connie's wedding, June 18, 1976.

CORNELIA (CONNIE) CALLAHAN

Our second child, Connie, was born April 7, 1953 when we were living in New London, Connecticut. Like Joe, Connie was born at Faulkner Hospital in Boston. and was five when we moved to Chagrin Falls. She went to a new high school called Glen Oak, which was started by the Sisters of Sacred Heart on the same campus as Gilmour. The two schools have now merged but Connie graduated in the first graduating class while it was still an all girls' school. In high school she was particularly talented in writing. Some of her writings were highly acclaimed. She was not very interested in math or the other sciences.

After high school I went around with her to various colleges that interested her. After Glen Oak she was leaning

Figure 31   Jeff and Connie Richards, 1990.

towards a coed school. However she was always very strong willed and conscious of sexual discrimination. She would ask if the men and women were treated equally. Of course we were always told there was no difference in treatment. Then Connie would ask who was the class president of each class. It was men. So she decided to go to Hollins College in Roanoke, Virginia which was all female except for about 15 men attending graduate school.

As it turned out, Connie started taking some graduate classes her junior and senior years and met her future husband, Jeff Richards. Jeff completed his Masters at Hollins College. They were married on June 18, 1976 and moved to Tuscaloosa, Alabama where Jeff continued postgraduate studies at the University of Alabama.

Connie has had an impressive business career for someone with a college education in the liberal arts. In

Tuscaloosa she decided to get a job in a Doctor's office. I think in applying she said she could type even though she had not bothered to learn to type up to that time. In typical manner she took charge of the office. She found that the doctor was billing the patient and also Medicare and then keeping both payments. Connie soon put a stop to it.

When Jeff and Connie moved to Washington DC, Connie went to work for Mr. Malarky, the owner of a cable TV consulting firm. Connie started off in charge of Accounts Receivable for the company. The owner of the company was very difficult to work for, always screaming and hollering at the employees. Connie would call me and I would encourage her to stick it out. She was soon office manager. At one time he promised everyone a bonus and then reneged when it came time to

Figure 32   Hannah at age 4.

71

Figure 33   Benjamin and Hannah about age 6.

pay. Connie stood up to him and demanded the bonus for the other employees. After that was secured she demanded her own bonus. After about a year her annual salary was up to $60,000.

When Connie decided to leave this job she pronounced herself a computer expert. She went around installing computer systems in all kinds of professional offices. I was really impressed and proud of her business acumen.

Jeff and Connie were in the process of adopting Benjamin when they found out Hannah was on the way. Benjamin was born May 28, 1989 and Hannah was born September 27, 1989. Hannah was born premature and weighed less than five pounds at birth. She is now almost as big as Benjamin. She is a very quiet, sweet girl. Benjamin is a straight A student. He is an outstanding soccer, baseball and basketball player. Looks like he is going to be an outstanding athlete.

Jeff is a college professor teaching primarily creative writing. Connie is full time mom and homemaker. They are both very dedicated to their children. They live in Takoma Park, Maryland and have a summer home on Martha's Vineyard.

TIMOTHY JOHN CALLAHAN

Our last child, Tim, was born February 28, 1956, almost a leap year baby, at the Boston Lying In Hospital. We were living in Arlington, Virginia at the time. When Tim was two we moved to Acton, Massachusetts and when he was three we moved to Chagrin Falls.

Tim was always a very busy young man, even in the second and third grades. He was interested in mechanical things and would follow me around the house anytime I was fixing something. In the sixth and seventh grades he was known as the "mad scientist" because he liked to experiment with his chemistry set. We jokingly said we

Figure 34   Tim about 1993.

always had his chemistry lab on the top floor of the house because that way he would only blow the roof off and not blow up the entire house. He became known as the leading rocketeer in town. The local toy store would refer customers to Tim as an expert in setting off rockets.

In high school he went to Gilmour Academy. He tried running cross country but developed back problems after running long distances. So he concentrated on his interest in photography and was the class photographer all four years of high school. They had a dark room in the basement of the high school and Tim would teach the other kids how to develop pictures. He was one of the editors for the school year book and took all the pictures. By using a time exposure he could set up the shot and then get in the picture. He liked wearing a large hat and horsing around with his friend Hubby Crowther.

Tim and Hubby started a house painting business their senior year of high school and first year of college. They only painted the interiors, not the outside. Tim was very meticulous and they had an excellent reputation for their work. Their clientele owned some of the better homes in town.

Because of his interest in photography, Tim decided to go to Rochester Institute of Technology in Rochester, New York. This is the leading photography school in the US. Eastman Kodak, Xerox and Bausch & Lomb were there and furnished the money to build the Institute. Tim had several exhibitions where he would show his pictures. When he graduated he was asked to stay and teach which he did for about eight years. He developed a reputation as someone who could do very good dye transfer work, which makes color photography archival, lasting hundreds of years. He did work for the Eastman Museum in Rochester and during the summers taught at the International School of Photography.

Tim also developed an interest in sound recording for television. When he left teaching he moved to Boston to work in television. He had purchased a top of the line, $70,000 16mm movie camera. On television crews he was qualified to be the cameraman or sound technician. He was part of the crew that did a special program on China for Public Television. It was five one-hour segments. He also was involved in filming Pavarotti in China for Public Television.

While he was a professor at Rochester Institute of Technology Tim became interested in one of his students, Debbie Bork. Debbie is very bright and a good athlete. She was born February 10, 1954 in Austin, Minnesota. She excelled as a gymnast in high school and now is in the

Figure 35   Tim and Deb with Margaret, Christmas 1987.

process of becoming a Class A tennis player. They were married May 27, 1985 in Cleveland, Ohio.

Their first child, Margaret, was born July 20, 1987. Like her Uncle Joe she has bright red hair. She also has the personality associated with a redhead being somewhat bossy and temperamental. She is also very bright, competitive in her school work and an excellent swimmer.

Figure 36   Margaret.

Figure 37   Caroline.

Their second child is Caroline, born February 10, 1989. Caroline swims like a fish. When she was five she walked over to the big pool at the country club, jumped in and started toward the deep end. The life guard told her she couldn't be in the big pool unless she could swim two lengths of the pool. So she did. Caroline is also a straight A student.

Their third child is TJ, born September 8, 1992. TJ, at age 6, is quieter than the girls, perhaps a bit shy still. He seems to be very smart in math and, after watching the girls

Figure 38   TJ.

play the piano, he gets up and plays. He may have a real talent for music. He is also interested in baseball and the rockets he and his dad shoot off. He has no fear of heights and sometimes his climbing escapades have been known to end in disaster. He has already broken a wrist in a climbing accident.

Debbie and Tim started reading to their kids at four months of age. They are both very dedicated to the kids, always taking them on trips to foreign countries and local

Figure 39   Debbie with Margaret and TJ.

cultural events.. Each of their children has a computer and learning programs. If they get behind in a subject they can use a computer program and make a game of learning the material.

Debbie was a grant administrator for archival photography at Rochester Institute of Technology. Now in Cleveland she has decided to keep doing something outside the home. So she is working a half day, three days a week at the Cleveland Clinic. Debbie is also very good at crafts and will often teach classes for the neighborhood kids on Saturdays. At Christmas they invite about 60 neighborhood kids and their parents to a party and she has the kids in the basement making all kinds of crafts on six different tables she sets up while the parents socialize upstairs. Tim and Debbie are well suited for each other because they are both very active and have a wide variety of interests.

Figure 40   With Mary about 1990.

In 1995 I hired Tim to manage my business interests. He completed the Executive MBA program at Case Western Reserve in June of 1999 and has become very knowledgeable and skilled in various technical investments.

With many challenges Mary and I have raised three children and now have seven grandchildren. Mary was always willing to put up with the agonies associated with being a diabetic. She wanted to have children and was willing to go through the special experimental treatments necessary. She coped bravely with the side effects from the fluoride treatments. Through it all she remained positive. She became involved in helping other diabetics learn to deal with the affliction. She would get angry with doctors who always blamed any of her other ailments on being a diabetic. For example, she had a hammertoe and the doctor said it was because of her diabetes. She asked, "Do any non diabetics have hammer toe?" The answer was "Yes." She would question, "Then how do you know mine is caused by diabetes?" Same with high blood pressure which the doctors blamed on her diabetes. Yet her father had high blood pressure and was not a diabetic.

Mary was very smart, a straight A student. She always had a great smile, liked to hear stories and jokes. She had a pleasant, fun-loving personality, liked to go to dances and parties and was active with the Cleveland Orchestra and Cleveland Institute of Music. She liked jewelry and pretty clothes and was very style conscious.

Mary loved to travel and wanted to see everything. We would fly to Europe and then drive through the different countries. We drove through England, Scotland and Ireland. Then on the continent we traveled through Holland, Germany, Norway and spent three weeks in France. We went to Hong Kong and Singapore several times and also Australia and New Zealand. The last six years of her life we began taking a cruise each year because her stamina was waning. On one cruise we sailed from Copenhagen to Stockholm up through all the fjords of Norway all the way past the Arctic Circle and then came back down and up the Thames River and under London Bridge. On another trip we sailed the Mediterranean, the Greek Isles and Turkey. We spent a lot of time in Greece looking at all the sites there.

Mary was also very interested in everything I was doing. She kept a scrapbook of clippings on all my achievements. She was very happy that I was selected for the Board of the Cleveland Clinic Foundation. She appreciated that as being quite an honor because her family was in medicine.

An interesting event occurred in 1976. We knew Jimmy and Rosie Carter because Jimmy and I had served together on the K-1 (Chapter 4) and he was one year behind me at the Academy. Mary was chairman of the fashion show fund-raiser for the Cleveland Orchestra the year Jimmy was running for president. Rosie was campaigning at a shopping center in Parma when it started raining. Mary had told Rosie that she would be in Severance Hall with the fashion show. When it started raining Rosie came in with all the secret service with her and said she wanted to see Mary Callahan. Mary got a big kick out of having her picture in the paper with Rosie Carter.

Right up to the end Mary was adamant about maintaining her independence and especially about driving the car. Through the years she had three or four insulin reactions while driving and ended up in the ditch several times. One accident came close to being bad but the other cars got out of her way. She was going down the wrong side of the road and smashed up the car by hitting a telephone pole. But fortunately no one was hurt. She was afraid the police would make her stop driving. However she was still driving in 1992 when she was stricken with her final illness. She had a stroke from which she did not recover.

Mary died July 16, 1992 at age 66. She had a lot of tough times. But because she faced the tough times with such courage she lived to enjoy the good times as well. We shared a deep, abiding love that began with that first dance at the Memorial Hall in Lima, Ohio, Christmas 1942. Our marriage produced three wonderful children, seven grandchildren and a lifetime of memories.

As I grieved the loss of Mary, I stayed busy. I was active running the company and did a fair amount of traveling to see our distributors. Mal Mixon and I started our investment banking operation, MCM (Mixon, Callahan and Mansour).

Through MCM we were buying small companies and traveling to meetings in conjunction with turning the new acquisitions around. I also became very much involved with the Cleveland Clinic serving on five committees: Executive, Research, Development, Marketing and Budget and Management Information Systems.

Also in that period of time, I guess people thought I was getting a little old and might not be around too long. So if they were going to give me an award they had better go ahead and do it. In 1994 and 1995 it seemed like I was getting an award from some organization in town about every three months or so.

And during this time Tim moved to Cleveland to start managing my personal business affairs. I wanted Tim to be involved in case I should have a stroke or something.

Figure 41   With Bob Hope at closing of Cleveland Stadium, 1994.

Figure 42   Receiving the Distinguished Fellows Award, 1996. Presented by Mal Mixon, Chairman of the Board, Cleveland Clinic Foundation.

Figure 43   Receiving the Philanthropist of the Year Award, 1996, presented by David Cerone, President Cleveland Institute of Music.

Looking back, I want to emphasize how proud I am of the way my three children have turned out. All three have led productive lives, established solid marriages and are doing a good job raising their kids. Much of the credit goes to my first wife, Mary, who maintained and reinforced strong family values during the times I was away on active duty with the Navy. All seven of the grandchildren, from Tricia the oldest to TJ the youngest, seem to have a real zest for living. I enjoy watching their life adventures unfold.

BARBARA SAVAGE

In July 1995 I was at a party at the Hunt Club and struck up a conversation with Barbara Savage. Barbara was someone I knew casually in Chagrin Falls. Her first husband had died of cancer in 1970 and her second husband, Sam Savage, died of cancer in 1982. Her only child, Billy Carothers, was by her first husband. We enjoyed each others

Figure 44   Barbara, November 1996, going to Army-Navy game.

Figure 45   Our wedding at Gilmour Academy Chapel October 10, 1996.

company that night at the Hunt Club and I asked her to go out with me.

We went to various things around town for about a year and a half. Especially enjoyable was going to Cleveland Indians baseball games that summer of 1995. In the Fall I got tickets for us to the Army-Navy football game. We had quite a few dates, going to movies and Cleveland Orchestra Concerts in the Winter and baseball games in the Spring and Summer.

On October 10, 1996 we were married. Barbara's son Billy, his wife Pat and their three children - Annie, KK and Will - were at.the wedding. Also Tim and Debbie and their three children - Margaret, Caroline and TJ - were at our wedding. I was scheduled to have an aorta operation so we postponed a long honeymoon. We had a brief honeymoon at the Ritz Carlton in Cleveland.

Barbara's son, Billy Carothers, was born February 24, 1953 in Cleveland, Ohio. He attended University School until his father died. He finished his senior year at Shaker High School, participating in soccer and wrestling. After graduation he attended Arizona State (Tempe) and the University of Denver. Billy married Pat Orosz on January 15, 1983. Pat was born February 1, 1952. She attended Beaumont High School in Cleveland and graduated from Cornell and later the University of Ithaca with a Masters Degree in Speech Therapy.

Billy is a partner in a real estate company in Cleveland. Pat works several days a week as a speech therapist and will occasionally give speeches to large groups of speech therapists.

Billy and Pat have three outstanding children. Their first

Figure 46   Pat Carothers,
Billy's wife.

Figure 47   Billy Carothers,
Barbara's son.

child, Annie, was born July 23, 1985. Annie is a very talented girl and plays the piano and clarinet. She loves swimming and ice skating. Annie also loves cooking and bakes cookies and muffins for us. She is now going to Gilmour where she is getting very good grades. A money making activity is baby sitting. She is in great demand and deposits her earnings in her bank account. She plans to go to Notre Dame and be a teacher.

Their second child, Kathryn, is known as KK. She was born October 12, 1987. KK is already known as an outstanding athlete in soccer, baseball, basketball and hockey skating. She also plays the piano and is an excellent student.

Their third child is Will, born May 10, 1990. Will, with coaching from his dad, is a good soccer player, baseball player and swimmer. He is showing real talent on the piano and excels in school.

Figure 48 Annie, Barbara's oldest grandchild.

Figure 49   KK & Will, Barbara's other two grandchildren.

After Barbara and I were married we started coming to Naples for the winter, January through May. In 1997 I was recovering from my operations and couldn't play as much golf as usual. So that was the period that I showed Barbara the area of Southwest Florida. Barbara's birthday is November 14th. It has become a tradition that we go to New York for Broadway plays for her birthday.

In June 1998 we went to Chester, England. Dave Cheetham was celebrating his 20th anniversary of being a distributor with our company. We stayed in a hotel in Chester, which is a very interesting town near Manchester, a walled city. Dave and I played in a local one day golf tournament. In September of 1998 Barbara and I took a three-week trip including a cruise so we could finally say we had a real honeymoon. We flew to Zurich, Switzerland.

Figure 50   Barbara in Naples with Gorilla.

Figure 51   Two pictures of Barbara on a recent cruise.

Then on to Turkey and caught the Seaboard Spirit, spent two weeks cruising the Mediterranean around the Greek Isles and through the Corinth Channel, up to Venice and down and around the Boot of Italy, ending up in Rome for three days. In November of 1998 we were, of course, back to New York for Broadway plays on Barbara's birthday. Our most recent trip was to the Julliard on January 26, 1999.

Barbara loves travel, clothes and toeless shoes. She is very conscious of how she looks and spends time getting

Figure 52   Barbara ready for a social event in Naples.

her hair and nails done and loves massages. It pays off because she has a great complexion to go with her great smile.

It is fun being with Barbara. She finds six or seven Valentines and one arrives every day for a week before Valentine's Day. Birthdays get the same kind of treatment with multiple presents. Besides this she likes football and baseball games and loves to watch and play tennis. I probably play too much golf to suit her but I warned her about that before we got married.

Barbara and I have enjoyed trips together and family dinners with her family and mine. We have grown closer through our marriage since October 10, 1996 and look forward to many more happy years together.

4

Galileo insisted on the supremacy of the "irreducible and stubborn facts" however "unreasonable" they may seem.

Naval Career - Submarine Duty

Submariner's Prayer

O God, it is rumored you're a little upset with submariners. They have the annoying habit of topping some of your finest efforts.

You walked on water. They found a way to walk under it. You divided the Red Sea amid noise and clamor, leaving behind a gaping wide trench. They divide the sea silently, leaving no trace at all. Then in one of your finest hours, when you were really on a roll, you took the first submariner, Jonah, submerged him in the sea for three days in the belly of a whale, and then dramatically let him live to tell the tale. Now these showoffs submerge themselves in their steel fish for months at a time, and without batting an eye, come home hale and hearty.

They are a determined lot, Oh Lord. I can understand your being testy; no one likes to be upstaged. But in your heart of hearts, I know You like their style. We are grateful for them in the Navy and I know You are too. The world is a better place, a freer place for what they do. They are the silent sentinels around the world. Bless those serving on lonely patrols this evening; unite in spirit with them. And grant these submariners your most special blessing.

Amen

Blessing presented at the Great Lakes Submarine Birthday Ball, April 24, 1982 by Chaplain Owen Melody LT CH USNR.

Graduating from the Naval Academy on June 6, 1945 I was granted my first choice of assignments which meant attending the four-month submarine school. The next school would start August 27. While waiting for the class to start the first order of business was a 30-day leave. I had proposed marriage to Mary Krouse and as noted in the last chapter we were married in Lima, Ohio on June 30 and then reported to Jacksonville, Florida for a one month Air Observer School. From there I reported on board the USS Cuttlefish (SS171) in New London, Connecticut on August 6, 1945 in preparation for Submarine School three weeks later.

In December 1945 I graduated submarine school 8th out of a class of 100. After graduation I attended a one-month Sonar and Radar Operator's School before reporting to the USS Grouper (SS 214). Grouper was an experimental radar picket submarine. It was basically a WW II Fleet boat with special electronic equipment installed to perform the Radar Picket function.

The USS Grouper (SS 214)

Figure 53   USS Grouper (SS 214) WW II Fleet Boat.

On February 16, 1946 as I reported on board the Grouper I made the "mistake" of turning on the radar set. Captain Charles Putnam, Class of '37, recognized this brilliant move and immediately named me the ship's Electronic Officer. There had not been an electronic technician aboard Grouper for several months and the equipment was in lousy condition. What made the situation worse was that the Grouper as an experimental Radar Picket Submarine could not conduct operations without the radio and radar gear working. Two days after getting this marvelous assignment by the Captain, none of the radars would work. The Captain's solution was to put me "In Hack" until they were working. "In Hack" meant that I could not leave the ship for any purpose.

I hauled out all the Radar Instruction books and began my study of electronics. This was exactly the learning technique that had been applied the past three years at the academy. I spent hours in the wardroom reading about circuits, test procedures, maintenance schedules, etc. Within a week I had all the Radars operating and was finally allowed to go ashore.

In addition to myself and Captain Putnam, the other officers on the Grouper were Ray Welch, XO, Class of '41, Len Cushing, Chief Engineer, Mustang, Bill Boose 1st Lt., Class of 44 and Bill Schuman, Communications, Class of '45.

The concept of a Radar Picket Submarine like the Grouper resulted from heavy losses of Destroyers on radar picket duty during WWII. Destroyers were deployed as a radar picket in advance of the main carrier task force. When the radar detected enemy aircraft closing on the task force they alerted the carriers which then had time to launch fighters. The fighter pilots were in communication with the radar picket destroyers and could be vectored in to intercept and destroy the incoming enemy planes. The Japanese retaliated with kamikaze attacks on the destroyers, which led to our equipping the Grouper with special radar and communications equipment to perform the radar picket function.. The concept was that submarines could dive and avoid the kamikaze attacks. This would break the intercept mission for a few minutes but at least lives and destroyers would not be lost performing the radar picket duty.

While aboard Grouper, I was sent to a CIC (Combat Information Center) school in Rhode Island for training as a Fighter Director Officer to learn how to order aircraft to intercept enemy aircraft.

On Grouper we practiced this type of operation including diving to avoid aircraft making simulated runs on us like a kamikaze would. I was one of the few CIC Fighter Director Officers in submarines.

In addition to Radar Picket Operations, the Grouper

participated in all routine submarine training exercises such as firing torpedoes and acting as target for destroyers making simulated depth charge and Y gun runs on enemy submarines.

I soon concluded that submarine-surface warfare was really a test of which fighting force had the greatest command of electronics. Radar could be used to find ships on the surface at considerable range. But Electronic Countermeasure Equipment could detect radar at an even greater range. The same was true of Pinging or Active Sonar. The target by listening could detect the pinging source further away than the active sonar could detect the submerged target. It appeared to me that the more I knew about electronics, the better I would be as a future submarine captain.

The Navy evidently had come to the same conclusion because they were continually requiring submarine officers to go to Radar or Sonar schools. After my name had been sent in to go to four months of Sonar school and two months of Radar School I decided that I and the Navy would be better served if I studied these subjects at MIT. My application to attend the Electrical Engineering Course in Naval Electronics at MIT was approved to begin January 15, 1947. In the meantime I continued with more training on the Grouper.

The Grouper was also serving as a school boat. That is, we took out sub school officers and students to help train them in submarine operations. We would go out and make 12 to 14 dives per day for training of sub school personnel. The only limit to the number of dives was the amount of high-pressure air needed to make the dives.

Between being a school boat and working out with destroyers as a submarine target, we put in a lot of long days. At the end of a week of this type of operations, we were proceeding up the Thames going into New London, when we received a message to go back out and pick up a sailor who had been injured aboard a destroyer in Long Island Sound.

We reversed course and went back out to sea. The sailor had his arm badly injured in a winch when they were recovering a boat. The ship from which we were to pick up the sailor was an old four-stack destroyer. I had the conn as we approached the ship and Captain Charley Putnam came up to the bridge and relieved me.

As we were maneuvering alongside, Charley ordered Port ahead two thirds and starboard back full. Our headway was still more than he wanted so he ordered Port back full, thinking that this would give him all back full. The problem was that starboard was going ahead full by mistake and, ahead being more efficient that astern, we proceeded to run the bull nose of the submarine across the well deck of the destroyer. This was a full-blown collision at sea.

My impression of the whole affair was that when the destroyer was hit its collision alarm sounded five fast blasts, rang up full speed and charged ahead on the engines. It was like a dog's tail being stomped on and the destroyer was yipping away as fast as she could go.

We finally got disentangled and the destroyer was not badly damaged. We had peeled the bow buoyancy tank back about ten feet which did not affect our surface operational ability. We picked up the injured sailor and returned to port.

Bill Boose and I stayed up all night to get the steel plate cut off of the bow buoyancy tank. The next morning we got underway to carry out our planned operations. At about 10:00 AM we were recalled and given hell for going out with a damaged submarine. As an ensign, I was not told a lot of what went on. But I don't think this whole operation added a lot to Charley Putnam's naval career.

The Grouper was ordered to Portsmouth Naval Shipyard at Kittery, Maine in December 1946. We went from New London, Connecticut via the Cape Cod Canal. Half way through the canal, a heavy fog set in and we were forced to anchor for the night. One of the sailors kept throwing a heaving line (a light line with a monkey fist on the end) against what sounded like a wooden wall. The next morning when the fog lifted we saw a house on the edge of the canal with black marks from the monkey fist all over it. There were about six windows on the side of the house and miraculously the monkey fist never hit a window. We lifted anchor and quietly left.

On January 15, 1947 I reported to MIT to obtain a degree in Electrical Engineering (Navy Electronics BSEE). I completed the degree in 20 months, graduating in September 1948. My training at the Academy stood me in good stead as I graduated with a GPA of 4.6 on a five point system. There were 27 courses, heavily weighted to Electrical Engineering and Communications but also including such courses as Economic Principles and Labor Relations. It was a very good 20 months. As I wrote in Chapter Three, son Joe was born December 27, 1946 so I was able to be home with him and Mary for that early period of his life. We lived on Beacon Street within walking distance of MIT.

The USS Volador (SS 490)

***Figure 54   USS Volador (SS 490)   First Guppy Submarine built from new
Hull and not a conversion from WWII Fleet Boat.***

Upon graduation I was ordered to Portsmouth Naval Shipyard as part of the Pre-commissioning Detail of the USS Volador (SS 490). Volador had not been launched as of the end of WW II and work had been stopped on her when the war ended. Later the Navy decided to complete the Volador as a new Guppy-Snorkel Submarine. Guppy stood for "greater underwater propulsion power." Volador could snorkel and recharge batteries without surfacing. It had a streamlined hull, could shift batteries to series and make about 18 knots submerged. Other boats such as Pickerel and Amberjack had been converted to Guppies from Wartime fleet submarines. Amberjack became famous for high-speed 45 degree up and down angles and earned the nickname "Anglejack".

Howie Thompson, Class of '39, was the Volador

Commanding Officer. His previous duty had been Commanding Officer of the Naval Prison at Portsmouth. The XO was Dick Schafer, '40; the Operations Officer was Andy Kemper, a Mustang (meaning he had received his commission from the ranks); the Engineering Officer was Rosie Roseanna, '44; the First Lt. was Larry Stahl, '46; the Supply Officer was Dick Colquhoum, '47; Dale Becker, '45 was Stores Officer. And I was Communications and Electronics Officer.

For a ship with only 65 sailors, we put together a great basketball team. Dick Colquhoun, Class of '47, had played on my Company team at Annapolis, played guard with a First Class Motor Machinist Mate. I played forward with the ship's Yeoman at the other side and our Chief Pharmacist Mate played Center. The Portsmouth Naval Base League consisted of six teams, including the Marines from the Naval Prison who had been league champions for the past seven years. However their winning streak ended in the 1948-49 season as Volador took the Championship.

The following season, 1949-50, we were in San Diego and champing at the bit to test ourselves in another basketball league. The only one available was the Big Ship League consisting of two aircraft carriers with 4,000 sailors each, two communications ships with 600 sailors each and a cruiser with a 1200 man complement. Our Captain, Howie Thompson thought we were crazy to get into this league against apparently superior teams and refused to come to any of the games although he had come to all of our games in Portsmouth.

I was out of shape and turning green running up and down the court. Mary thought I would drop dead at any minute. Nevertheless we ended up playing the Aircraft Carrier Valley Forge for the league championship. They finally beat us in two overtimes. We claimed to have the best submarine team in the Navy. There were no challengers.

We left Portsmouth in March 1949 and proceeded to Norfolk, Key West, New Orleans, Houston and through the Panama Canal en route to San Diego. On the eastern end of the Canal we were headed to a degaussing station to have our magnetic field minimized. The station was off the beaten path, outside the channel, and we managed to go aground in 9 feet of water. We drew 16 feet. With high tide and the help of couple of large sea tugs we were able to get off the rock and proceed to the degaussing station.

Several months later we were practicing 45 degree down and up angles while making high speed, 18 knots, submerged. Suddenly we lost control of the boat and began plunging into the depths. It was a terrifying moment for all on board. We began emergency procedures of blowing bow buoyancy, all ballast tanks and backing down with full power on the screws. Finally at 600 feet we leveled off. Nothing seemed so slow as this blow, although we probably stopped the downward momentum in about 20 very long seconds.

To understand the terror of the moment I need to introduce some math. The rule of thumb for converting speed in knots to speed in yards per minute is to simply divide the knots by three and multiply by 100. So 18 knots becomes 600 yards per minute (18 divide by 3 times 100). 600 yards per minute is the same as 10 yards per second (divide yards per minute by 60) or 30 feet per second (convert yards to feet). So at 18 knots we are moving through the water at 30 feet per second. Now on a practice 45 degree descent at 18 knots our increased depth would be .707 times 30 or 21.2 feet per second. We would normally begin our practice descent from a depth of 100 feet. To reach test depth of 412 feet would only take about 15 seconds

(312 divided by 21.2). So we were used to a controlled 15 second descent. Out of control we plunged 500 feet in 20 seconds. Those extra five seconds were especially long.

Another rather exciting event occurred while we were on fleet maneuvers in the Pacific. We were attempting to penetrate the screen of the task force protecting the Valley Forge, a large aircraft carrier. The task force was zigzagging at about 32 knots and we had maneuvered to get on the track of the carrier. We were at battle stations and conducting a simulated submerged night attack on the Valley Forge. The task force was traveling "darkened ship". We had generated a solution that the carrier was at 32 knots with a zero angle on the bow and we were headed directly at her at about four knots. Our relative speed was 36 knots. Using the conversion rule of thumb, we were closing at 1200 yards per minute (36 divided by 3 times 100).

The Captain put the scope up trying to see the Valley Forge. The radar in the periscope gave us a range of 1200 yards. At this rate we would collide with the monster in one minute. As the seconds continued to tick the Captain kept trying to see the Valley Forge in the dark to get an angle on the bow. When the range on the Torpedo Data Computer (TDC) got down to 700 yards, I hollered in a not too respectful tone, "For God's sake Captain, let's get down, the range is 700 yards!" (Shades of Sweet Talking Brown which you will hear about in Chapter Seven.)

Finally the Captain ordered, "Flood Negative, all ahead full, take her down to 200 feet." The length of the Valley Forge passed overhead with about 10 feet to spare. With her 32 ' draft and 32 knots, she vibrated the whole submarine. Other boats in somewhat similar conditions had their periscopes and radar antennas bent over by collision with the bottom of the surface ship. At 700 yards and a closure rate of 1200 yards per minute, we were within 35 seconds of smashing the giant aircraft carrier head on.

The flares we fired from the signal gun, to indicate that we had fired simulated torpedoes, landed on the deck of the Valley Forge. The quartermaster said the Captain had Navy Crosses in his eyes as he kept us at periscope depth so long with the target closing.

After about 18 months on Volador Eugene P. (Dennis) Wilkinson relieved Howie Thompson as Captain. Dennis was later to become the first Commanding Officer of Nautilus and make history as the Captain of the first ship ever to get "Underway on Nuclear Power."

Shortly after Dennis came aboard, I applied to become the Engineering Officer on the Nautilus. This was probably in April or May of 1950 before the keel had been laid or the prototype built. I was already interested in nuclear power.

While serving under Dennis Wilkinson, we had several Operational Readiness Inspections (ORI) and made many airless surfaces practicing for these ORI's. A normal surface is made by coming to periscope depth, look around to make sure no one is going to run you down if you surface, then blow water out of the tanks by blowing with high pressure air. Once on the surface, the upper and lower conning tower hatches are opened, the low pressure blower is started and it finishes blowing water out of the tanks before the main induction is opened.

An "airless surface" assumes the submarine had been submerged for a period of time and had used up or lost all high pressure air. Like with a normal surface, you plane up to periscope depth and look around. If all clear you plane up to the surface, put the bow planes on RISE and the stern planes on DIVE and run at about 5 knots. Both planes act to give lift and keep the submarine on the surface. Once you have established a steady condition in this manner, you open the upper and lower conning tower hatch and start the low pressure blowers to blow the water out of the tanks. My airless surface training on the Volador would be critical on a subsequent assignment.

Also with Dennis Wilkinson and the Volador we practiced a mine plant. The goal was to lay a full load of 60 mines in a perfect pattern. We had ten torpedo tubes and would shoot six mines from each tube. The trick was getting the mines loaded on time so that the proper pattern could be dropped. If all went well you had a set sequence that was optimum for the mine plant. If you did not have a forward tube ready on time, you could shoot a stern tube about a minute later and still put a mine in the exact position. The trick was to always be ready to shoot a stern tube mine in case the bow tube had not been loaded. I figured out a complicated system that kept a stern tube always loaded to correct for a late load on the bow tubes.

As we were preparing to shoot a mine plant, I explained my system to Dennis. He replied, "I don't know what you are talking about, but it had better work." It did and we were complimented for being the only boat to ever lay a perfect plant from the San Diego squadrons.

In June 1950 I took my first 30 day leave. With Mary and little Joe we drove from San Diego to Lima. We had been home about three days when I received orders to report back to the Volador in Pearl Harbor because the Korean War had started. I left Mary and Joe with the car in Lima and headed to Pearl. I was delayed several weeks in San Francisco waiting for air transportation to Pearl as other branches of the service had higher priority to get to Korea.

Upon arriving in Pearl, I learned that the Volador had orders to go on patrol. We were to load war heads on all torpedoes, take on stores for ninety days and proceed to patrol station off Vladivostok. While we were making preparations we were sent to sea for a final inspection. On the way back into Pearl, the Chief Radioman came to the bridge and said that I had orders to report to the Sterlet in Mare Island Naval Shipyard. I thought he was pulling my leg. After we docked I went to base radio and asked if such a message had come in over the fox schedule. It was confirmed.

Dennis called me to his cabin while he was making out my departure fitness report. He asked me, "Do you intend to make the Navy your career?" I replied honestly. "If I get the assignments I want and if I enjoy what I am doing, I will stay in. If I don't, I'll get out." I suspect that most senior naval officers would have given me a black mark for making such a statement. So I watched with a little surprise as he wrote on my fitness report, "and he is a very intelligent young man."

As the last of the original commissioning crew of the Volador to leave the ship, I was the plank owner. The commissioning plaque was taken down and given to me. Dennis had the boatsman pipe me over the side when I left. And so I missed patrol off Russia.

The USS Sterlet (SS 392)

On August 26, 1950 I reported aboard the USS Sterlet (SS 392) at Mare Island Naval Shipyard. Sterlet was a WW II "Fleet Boat" which had been placed in 'moth balls' after

Figure 55   USS Sterlet (SS 392).

the war. Three to four hundred of this standard design had been built during the war. Now with the start of the Korean War I was ordered to be part of the crew that would take her out of the mothball fleet and make fully operational in 30 days. We took the Sterlet out within 30 days. It was the first boat out of mothballs and the only one to start operating after 30 days. All following boats were allowed 65 days based on our experiences. En route from Mare Island naval Shipyard to San Diego, the boat still leaked like a sieve. We affectionately referred to her as "Sterlet the Terlet, not to be confused with toilet!"

The crew had been requisitioned from other boats which were asked to send certain rates for reactivating the Sterlet. Consequently we seemed to receive crew members that the other boats wanted to get rid of. Generally they all were well qualified in their rates, but they had a history of not being the best when they were ashore. As long as they were kept at sea, they were fine.

The officers were better. Our Captain was George

Kittredge, Class of '40. He made war patrols during WW II but did not have recent duty in submarines and was a little rusty. At the end of WW II he was the XO on the Grouper. The skippers who had fought a tension packed war were flown home and XO's like George were left to bring the boat back home. After the war George became Naval Attaché in India and played polo with the Maharajahs! He refused to take submarine duty because the detail desk wanted to make him executive officer and he claimed he had already been Captain when he brought the Grouper back from the Pacific. So we got George with no submarine operations from 1945 to 1950.

Chuck Tisdale, Class of '44, was twin brother of a class mate of mine, Robert Tisdale. Chuck graduated from sub school about two years after I had. After about a year of submarine duty he had gone to Commander Submarine Force Pacific Fleet (ComSubPac) and taken a staff position. He became our Chief Engineer and Diving Officer and did not have much operating experience.

My classmate, Ansel Braseth, had about four years experience riding boats as I had and was a welcomed addition to the crew.

Hal Howard, Class of '42, was assigned as Executive Officer. Hal did not impress me as very strong, but when the chips were down he had a lot of reserve strength.

Our Supply Officer was Chuck Rauch, Class of '48, a chubby Ensign fresh out of sub school. Chuck was not overly impressive at the time but he went on to make Admiral in charge of integration of the races in the Navy. Showing true dedication to the cause, Chuck divorced his wife, who was white, and married his secretary who was black.

We were a motley crew as we gathered at Mare Island Naval

Shipyard, north of San Francisco and proceeded to work 16 hour days to put the Sterlet back into sea going condition.

After only two weeks of testing systems alongside the dock, we got underway and made our first dive. At a depth of 60 feet we were taking on water from about 200 leaks. We returned to port, spent two days tightening packings and went back to sea. At a depth of 100 feet we found 60 new leaks. About this time we were not at all sure we had a great boat. We tried compartment pressure tests and could not pass any of them. At least the high pressure air system valves worked and we could try to build up pressure in the individual compartments.

In a shaky state of readiness, we departed San Francisco at the end of 30 days and proceeded to San Diego where I had qualified for Command in Submarines during my almost two years operating on the USS Volador (SS 490). San Diego was a high class readiness operation . Our Operational Inspections and Administrative Inspections were the best I had experienced.

We trained daily at sea, going through ship drills to bring our crew up to submarine operating standards. The tides were tricky and tying up to the tenders took a bit of skill. For the first two weeks, Captain Kittredge had me make the landings since I had made many landings while on the Volador. Finally George got up enough nerve to try it himself. He proceeded to hit the screws of the USS Redfish, putting her out of commission for several weeks.

While on watch one Saturday shortly after arrival in San Diego, three of the crew who had been on shore leave came back aboard earlier than expected. They reported that the Captain had seen them in town in civilian clothes and had sent them back to the ship under arrest. During WW II all military personnel were required to be in uniform at all times while in public. But the rule had long since changed and soldiers, sailors and airmen were allowed to wear civilian clothes while ashore. I sent the crew members back on shore leave and told them I would take care of it.

About 16:30 Captain George arrived on board and wanted to know where his prisoners were. I told him that I had sent them back ashore as the wearing of uniforms ashore had not been required for five years. Of course I had to dig out the Naval District Order to prove the "new" regulation. So much for an isolated Naval Attaché.

As we proceeded with our readiness training, George recognized that the crew and officers did not trust the integrity and tightness of the Sterlet. While we were out at sea one day, he decided we should go to test depth and prove the boat was seaworthy.

George ordered, "Take her down to 400 feet" after everyone was at battle stations. At 275 feet, the report came from the forward room, "the Pressure hull has cracked". I quickly went forward, looked through the water tight door and saw water spraying all over the forward torpedo room. I called to the control room, "Surface! Surface!"

When we got up, we discovered a grease line to the JT sonar had been disconnected. When the pressure rose high enough it blew the grease out and sprayed water all over the forward Torpedo Room. What made it scary was that masking tape had been used to cover over the connection and the interior hull had been spray painted so that the water looked like it was coming right through the hull.

About a week later we returned to port on a Thursday. On Friday the XO, Hal Howard, gave leave to about six of the crew so they could go to San Francisco and bring their families to San Diego. The crew members were going over the gangway when Captain George saw them. When told they were granted leave he countermanded his XO saying, 'Cancel their leave. We are firing a torpedo today." So the sailor's wives and children had checked out of their quarters and were left hanging when their husbands did not show up. Hal turned to the Captain and said, "From now on Captain, you grant all liberties and leaves. I will not handle it any longer." Good for Hal.

I had a similar confrontation with the Captain around November, 1950. A liner failed in one of our main engines. In reviewing the machinery history records left us by the de-commissioning detail, I determined that the failed liner and one other were known to be worn and they had not been able to get replacements. Indications were that all other cylinder liners were brand new. So I ordered the replacement of just those two liners.

The Chief Motor Machinist disagreed. He wanted to replace all the liners. He said he did not trust the people who put the boat into mothballs and thought we should overhaul the engine and replace all the liners, a very expensive operation. I went over it again, explained why I had decided that only two liners needed to be replaced and finally said, "Chief, that's an order and I don't want to hear any more about it."

Thirty minutes later I am in the wardroom having lunch with the Captain and other officers. The Chief Motor Machinist came in with the Machinery History Book and asked me again about replacing all the liners. I said, "Chief, we have already settled this. Do what I told you."

At that point the Captain butts in and says, "What's wrong Chief?" The chief explained his position and George countermanded my orders and said, "Go ahead and overhaul the engine and replace the liners."

After the Chief left, I said, "Captain that is your engine from now on."

Later we were in upkeep and all the liners had been removed and placed on the deck. The squadron engineer, Ray Welch (my XO from Grouper), called me up on deck and said, "Joe, why are you replacing all these brand new liners? We had to get a special allotment to pay for this engine overhaul and these parts are all new."

I replied, "Ray, that engine belongs to the Captain. Talk to him."

One of the biggest scares of my life occurred about a month later when George screwed up an "airless surface". I explained on page 104 about practicing the airless surface on the Volador with Dennis Wilkinson. It is the prescribed method to surface a submarine when you have lost or used up your high pressure air. Because part of the process is opening the hatch after obtaining a steady condition but before being fully emerged, there is a danger of flooding the boat.

Since I had been on several Operational Readiness Inspections on Volador and had practiced 10 or 15 airless surfaces I cautioned George to make sure we were up and planing on the surface for about 30 seconds before he opened the hatch. I also cautioned Chuck Tisdale to make sure the stern planes were on DIVE.

The Stern Planesman left the stern planes on RISE and the

Captain opened the hatch as soon as we broke the conning tower out of the water. We started down again with the upper and lower conning tower hatches open. The conning tower began flooding with water with the Captain, the Executive Officer, the Quartermaster and Chief Electronic Technician still inside. I grabbed the lanyard on the lower hatch as water was pouring in and pulled it shut while hollering, "Blow all Main Ballast!" The Chief on the air manifold froze so I went over and opened the forward and aft main ballast tank blow valves. We went to the surface as quickly as we could, opened the conning tower drain and commenced draining the conning tower. We had no communications with the conning tower and did not know if the Captain and others had drowned. After about ten minutes, we were able to open the lower hatch. An air bubble had formed at the rear of the conning tower and all four were able to keep their heads above water. They were scared and soaked, but OK. All the sonar and radar equipment were flooded but that did not seem important.

One other interesting assignment occurred on the Sterlet. We were volunteered to participate in the submarine movie, Submarine Command starring Nancy Olson, William Holden, Don Taylor and William Bendix. Two scenes were particularly memorable. One was when we put a raft over the side with the commandos who were going ashore to blow up enemy facilities. The other was when the submarine was hit by shore batteries and we abandoned ship.

In the commando scene, Bill Bendix played the Chief of the Boat. He was always blustering around on deck, giving orders and thinking up ways he could hog the camera. After the director told Bendix to stick to the script, they were able to get the inflated boat into the water and seven marines were sent on their way.

In the abandon ship scene it was supposed to be daylight but it was shot at night alongside the dock with many searchlights and cameras. The movie company offered any sailor who would jump over the side $50. I had the watch and would dive the boat alongside the dock to simulate a sinking submarine in distress. I kept everyone on board until we had rigged for dive and checked the rig. Then I let all but six go topside and jump so they could make the fifty bucks.

After about two weeks of shooting, the movie company threw a big party at the Del Coronado Hotel for all the stars and the officers and chiefs from the submarine. We were treated to cocktails, dinner, a band and dancing. I danced with Nancy Olson and trampled her toes a bit.

I was detached from the Sterlet on February 19, 1951 after a long six months. The next time I heard of George was when the Tall Ships came to New York on the 200th anniversary of U.S. Independence, July 4, 1976. George was manufacturing two man submarines. For publicity he steered one in amongst the big ships and caused quite a commotion. It's a wonder someone didn't sink him. The maneuver made all the New York papers.

George had been writing children's books about horses while on the Sterlet. Perhaps playing polo in India with the Maharajahs gave him ideas for short children's books about horses. I understand some were published. The last time I heard from him was about 1982. He was in the hospital and decided to call me at work. My secretary, Diane, answered. George said, "Is Mr. Callahan in?" She replied, "Yes." George said, "Tell him the pressure hull has cracked. He'll know who it is."

I took five days leave on February 19 and was detached from the Sterlet. That gave us eight days to travel cross country

Figure 56   USSK-1 (SSK-1) First Hunter-Killer Submarine.

in the Mercury Coup and report on February 27, 1951 to the Commissioning Detail of the USS K-1 (SSK-1) at Electric Boat in New London, Connecticut.

The USS K-1 (SS K-1)

The K-1 was the first of a possible new class of submarines. It was a small submarine with a crew of only 38 and was designed to be mass produced for a short war. There were six commissioned officers aboard this 950 ton, Hunter-Killer Submarine. Frank Andrews was the CO; Roy Cowdrey was XO; Charlie Woods was 1st Lt.; Jimmy Carter was Engineering Officer; Al Cohen was Supply and Commissary Officer; I was the Operations Officer. Jimmy Carter, in his book *Why Not the Best*, [page 52] stated that in January 1950 he reported "as Senior Officer of the pre-commissioning detail ….and was also responsible for the evolution of the

Figure 57 *L-R: Frank Andrews, Charlie Woods, Jean Andrews,*
Jimmy Carter, Bets Woods, Roy Cowdrey, Mary Callahan,
Joe Callahan, and Rosie Carter.

various procedures which would be used when the ship
ultimately went to sea, including engineering, maintenance,
diving and surfacing, development of personnel billets, and
projected supply requirements".

Frank Andrews and the other officers who began reporting
to the K-1 the following month - February - were all Senior
to the young future President and may perceive Jimmy's
statement to be somewhat exaggerated. However Jimmy
served admirably as a fellow crew member until he left to go
to KAPL (Knolls Atomic Power Lab) to train in Nuclear
Power for possible assignment as Engineer on the Seawolf.
His father died and he resigned from the Navy about six
months after he left K-1.

Figure 58   K-1 Crew. I am in front, in uniform as Duty Officer of the Day.

At the same time we were getting acquainted with the K-1, Ned Beach was on the New Construction Detail of the USS Tang and had offices connecting to ours. He later became renown for writing Run Silent, Run Deep, being a presidential naval aide to President Eisenhower and Commander of the USS Triton (SSRN 586) on its around the world submerged voyage. (On Rickover's staff I had spent a year on the design of the Triton.)

When we took the K-1 out for sea trials, we rode as observers. The boat was operated by civilian test crews who were employees of Electric Boat. They were not skilled submariners. We were scared to death riding with them. The use of a civilian test crew on boats before being commissioned was left over from World War II when experienced naval crews for testing were in short supply. We strongly recommended that the practice be discontinued and that the Navy Pre-commissioning Detail operate the boats on all trials. This recommendation was accepted and the K-1 was the last boat to use a civilian submarine crew for sea trials.

The K-1 had snorkeling ability and main power was three "dinky" engines of 450 HP each, producing a total shaft horsepower of about 1350 SHP. On the WW II fleet boats we had four diesels of 1500 HP each or 6,000 SHP. Maximum surface speed for the K-1 was 10 knots and the best submerged speed was barely six knots.

The purpose of this boat was to *hunt* and *kill* enemy submarines. To accomplish this mission, K-1 had the newest in listening (passive) and pinging (active) sonar. The listening sonar was an array about 30 feet long in half an ellipse that was mounted along the starboard and port sides and around the bow. It was composed of about 120 hydrophones that were about 12 feet long mounted vertically. Each hydrophone could be time delayed so that the equivalent of a directional listening beam was formed. This was a major improvement over the JT, the standard World War II listening sonar which was a single, six foot long, horizontal hydrophone that was rotated by a shaft through the hull.

As one might guess, the K-1's massive array could detect the sound of other ships much further away than the single hydrophone used during WW II. In fact, the JT was considered to have a maximum range of about 10,000 to 11,000 yards and often would not hear a target until it reached a range of one or two thousand yards. The array on K-1 could hear the same target under the same conditions out to range of 60 miles or over 120,000 yards.

This ability to hear at long distances caused us a lot of trouble. No one would believe that we could hear at these distances and assumed we had over-active imaginations. The fact was, we could hear very well at these ranges and ships' propellers sounded like steam locomotives in a railroad station. We tried to explain to ComSubLant and ConSubDevGroup II that we couldn't go to battle stations whenever we made a contact. We would be at battle stations all the time. We could always hear somebody.

As the ship's Data Computer Operator, I worked with Captain Frank Andrews and Charlie Woods on the problem. We developed a method of ranging that we called the "lighthouse effect". If you are a long distance from a lighthouse, you can run at 15 knots with the lighthouse on your beam for 10 minutes and not observe a significant bearing change. If you were closer, say 6,000 yards from the lighthouse, and did the same thing, the bearing change would be close to 40 degrees. When we recommended this as a standard fire control procedure for estimating distance and determining when to go to battle stations, ComSubLant paid no attention to it. At my suggestion, Jimmy Carter wrote his command thesis explaining our theory and its practical application. A study of this type was required before a naval officer would be granted "Command of Submarines" status. My thesis had been *The World We Live In* (a technical discussion of sonars and the effects of noise and water conditions in the sonar equation) when I was serving on the USS Volador.

While serving on the Volador, I had applied to be Chief Engineer aboard Nautilus. My former skipper, Howie Thompson, was then in BuPers at the Submarine Desk after his tour as Captain of the Volador. He informed me that I was in the final three, but fell a little short because I did not have enough sea time. My sea time was interrupted by the twenty months I was at MIT between service on the Grouper and the Volador. Les Kelly, a classmate of mine got the selection. I continued to be interested in nuclear power while on the K-1 and that influenced Jimmy Carter to apply for an engineering officer job on the Seawolf.

I mentioned that K-1 had "dinky" engines which is the name given to them in WW II when all submarines had one as an auxiliary engine. They had the reputation of being extremely unreliable and were usually not operational. We found out why on the K-1. Large angle diving had become popular on all "guppy" boats. As a result, on K-1 we had to try 45 degree dives. They always gave me a terrified sinking feeling in the pit of my stomach, but as an officer I had to act like it was nothing. The only problem was that the "dinkies" did not have an oil seal between the engine sump and the electric generator it was driving. As a result, when we made steep dives of 45 degrees on K-1, we dumped oil from the oil sumps into the generators, grounding out the main generators.

About the same time, we discovered that we had full grounds on our main motors. This had been a problem on the old "S" boats but had been solved by putting electrostatic precipitrons on the DC motors which collected the carbon and prevented grounding of the main motors. Only problem was this cheap, mass produced K class was deemed not to need precipitrons because the war it was supposed to fight would be so short there would be no time for carbon build-up. Everyone - ComSubLant, BuShips, ComSubDevGroup II - had forgotten this. When I relieved Jimmy Carter as Chief Engineer on K-1 I discovered that the main motors and main generators had full grounds on them. Later an investigation was held and I explained the problem to a Board of Inquiry.

When Jimmy was elected President I sent him this telegram:

Dear Jimmy:

Who would have ever thought that the junior officer I relieved on K-1 with full grounds on all main generators and main motors would ever be elected President?"

I didn't receive a reply while he was in the White House. However, Mary and I were in contact from time to time. Below is a letter I received in 1993.

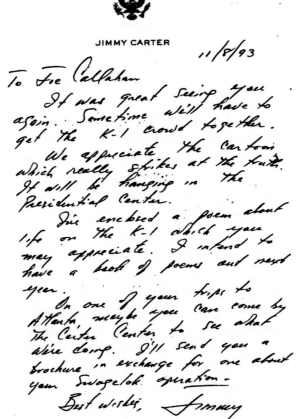

JIMMY CARTER 11/8/93

To Joe Callahan

It was great seeing you again. Sometime we'll have to get the K-1 crowd together.

We appreciate the cartoon which really strikes at the truth. It will be hanging in the Presidential Center.

I've enclosed a poem about life on the K-1 which you may appreciate. I intend to have a book of poems out next year.

On one of your trips to Atlanta, maybe you can come by the Carter Center to see what we're doing. I'll send you a brochure in exchange for one about your Swagelok operation—

Best wishes, Jimmy

Figure 59   Letter from former President Jimmy Carter, a crewmate on the K-1.

Here is the poem Jimmy mentioned in his letter.

Life on a Killer Submarine

By Jimmy Carter

I had a warm, sequestered feeling deep beneath the sea, moving silently, assessing what we could hear from far away because we ran so quietly ourselves, walking always in our stocking feet. We'd listen to the wild sea sounds, the scratch of shrimp, the bowhead's moan, the tantalizing songs of humpback whales. We strained to hear all other things, letting ocean lenses bring to us the oscillating beat of screws, the murmurs of most distant ships, or submarines that might be hunting us. One time we heard, with perfect clarity, a vessel's pulse four hundred miles away and remembered that, in spite of everything we did to keep our sounds suppressed, the gradient sea could focus, too, our muffled noise, could let the other listeners know where their torpedoes might be aimed. We wanted them to understand that we could always hear them first and, knowing, be inclined to share our love of solitude, our fear that one move, threatening or wrong, could cost the peace we yearned to keep, and kill our hopes that they were thrilled like us to hear the same whale's song.

We asked for help in repairing the main motors and main generators from the New London Sub Base Engineering and Repair Department. They came to the conclusion that we would need to go to a shipyard, open the hull and remove the main motors because there was not room to remove the field coils from the main motors from inside the ship. Comdr. Phil Beshamy, the Base Engineer and Repair Officer, made the recommendation to ComSubLant to send us to a shipyard.

That night I had the duty and asked the Captain if I could give a try at removing the Field Coils and maybe repair the motors alongside the dock. Frank Andrews said go ahead and give it a try.

The next morning we had all the coils on the dock and I called Cdr. Phil Beshamy and asked him to come down and pick them up. This was a great embarrassment to him and he did not appreciate what I had done.

About two weeks later when I again had the duty we received a horrible film for the duty crew to watch. The movie was supplied by the Base Engineering and Repair Department. As Duty Officer it was my responsibility to report on incidents during my watch. I reported that the movie was horrible and an insult to the Submarine Force to even distribute it.

Cdr. Beshamy took this as a second insult from me to his command and reported me to SubDevGroup II for insubordination. The Captain managed to get it squelched.

In the small world department, about twenty years later I was getting ready to tee off at Mayfield Country Club in Cleveland. I saw a Rear Admiral in full Navy Blues with Submarine Dolphins above his campaign bars. It was none other than Admiral Phil Beshamy. He was married to the sister of John and Bill Calfee, eminent lawyers in the City of Cleveland. I went over and introduced myself as a USNA graduate, class of '46 and a submariner. He apparently did not remember me as well as I remembered him, which was a blessing for both of us.

On the K-1, in order to hear the maximum distance it was important to be submerged and motionless - dead in the water.

To do this we had to displace water with the exact mass as that of the boat. This may seem easy but the slightest miss-match would cause the boat to go up or down. Once momentum was started it was difficult to stop. To stop the momentum an over correction was necessary and then another over correction the other way, and so on. All these corrections of flooding or pumping made noise and were undesirable for the best listening platform.

We discovered a solution that apparently no one had thought of before and subsequently became experts at hovering. Once we were submerged and had a good trim, at zero speed, we would continually monitor the pressure gauge and at the first indication of motion we would compensate with the snorkel mast. If we were going down we would raise the mast about three inches thereby slightly increasing our displacement. If we were going up we would retract the mast about three inches. Following these procedures we were able to keep the submarine at a consistent depth for hours on end.

I have always been a light sleeper. This may have saved the life of our future president as well as the rest of the crew. Al Cohen had the conn and made a dive. The noise of the air bleeding into the boat as we took a three degree down angle woke me up. I drifted back asleep. Then at some point I woke up with the uneasy feeling that we had been in the down angle for too long. I got up in my skivvies and went into the control room to see what was going on. Al had a four degree down angle and 2/3 speed. He said it appeared we had a heavy thermal layer and he could not get below 60 feet. The diving depth gauge indicated 60 feet. I looked at the pressure gauge on the fuel tank and saw that it was reading 220 pounds. Fuel tanks are open at the bottom so that the tank's pressure gauge reads sea pressure. There are approximately 44 pounds of pressure per 100 feet of sea water, so we were at about 500 feet and going down. The test depth or maximum safe depth is only 412 feet. I told Al to blow all main ballast. We were at 600 feet before we finally started going back up. Someone had closed the sea valve that supplied sea water to the diving pressure gauges. Sometimes a light sleeper is an asset.

My final dive on the K-1 was a harrowing experience. I had been selected by Rickover to go to MIT for a Masters in Nuclear Engineering and then to serve on his staff at Bureau of Ships. Captain Frank Andrews gave me the honor of making my last dive on K-1.

On the Bridge, I ordered, "Clear the Bridge" for the lookouts and the quartermaster to go below. As the OD, Officer of the Deck, I would be the last to go below for the dive. I then sounded the diving alarm, announced "Dive, Dive" over the 1MC, General Announcing System and got in the chute. I pulled the upper hatch shut and to my consternation it would not close. The ship was going down and I couldn't get the hatch shut. The lower hatch was still open waiting for me. With my fog horn voice I hollered down, "FOULED HATCH! CLOSE THE LOWER HATCH! As soon as the lower hatch was closed I opened the upper hatch and went back on deck ready to go over the side. Fortunately Charlie Woods was able to stop the dive with only 10 feet of water over the deck. We were able to get back on the surface and get properly ready for another dive.

So my being part of Ship's Crew on submarines ended. I had done a lot in my eight year career in submarines to that point. I had been on the first experimental Radar Picket Submarine in an old WW II Fleet Boat; on the first Guppy Snorkel built as a new boat; took the first WW II Fleet boat out of mothballs; and served on the first Hunter Killer Submarine with a future President of the USA. On the not so good side, I had been aground in the Volador; in a collision on the Grouper; had a flooded conning tower on the Sterlet; and finished up almost diving with an open hatch on the K-1.

It was a memorable eight years. I was now ready for my one year of shore duty at MIT in preparation for Nuclear Submarines and Admiral H. G. Rickover.

5

There is nothing as uncommon as common sense.

Naval Career - Nuclear Submarines

The potential of a true submersible, a submarine that could stay submerged indefinitely and could operate at full power without consuming oxygen, interested me early in my submarine career. As related on page104. I applied in 1950 to be Chief Engineer Officer aboard the first nuclear submarine. The program had been approved and money appropriated for what would become Nautilus. I continued to be intrigued by the potential of nuclear power.

On June 14, 1952, the K-1 was anchored in the channel with several other submarines at New London, Connecticut. I was standing on the deck of the K-1 in full dress whites when President Harry Truman struck a welding arc to symbolize the keel laying of the Nautilus. Later that evening we attended a celebration party hosted by Electric Boat Company at the Lighthouse Inn. I resolved again to apply for the nuclear submarine program.

It was about six months later that my application reached the final hurdle, THE INTERVIEW. If I were selected I would attend MIT for a Masters in Advanced Nuclear Engineering. The date of the interview was on Saturday November 29, 1952. On the train from New London, I met Sam Bassett, a classmate of mine who was serving at the Underwater Sound Lab in New London. He was also on his way to Washington for an interview with Captain Rickover. At that time Rickover had not yet been promoted to Admiral. We compared notes in anticipation of meeting the much-heralded Rickover.

Each candidate was interviewed by about five of Rickover's staff. The interviews by the staff were routine. Those who made the finals were interviewed by the great man himself. That interview was anything but routine.

Rickover started by asking the names of books I had read in the last six months. Who wrote each book? Why didn't I read more? In his opinion most of the books I had read were trash.

Next he asked me where I had gone to high school. When I told him that I had gone to Saint Rose in Lima, Ohio he wanted to know why it was called Saint Rose. I replied that Saint Rose was the Patron Saint of Lima Peru. And thus the church and school in Lima, Ohio were named Saint Rose. He said, "Are you sure of that?"

I replied, "Yes."

He then called his secretary in and said, "Get me the Peruvian Ambassador on the phone." As she hurried off he looked back at me and said, "Are you sure of what you just told me? Does it worry you that I am going to check with the Ambassador?"

I said, "No. I'm not worried."

After talking on the phone and confirming the origin of the name Saint Rose, he asked where I stood in my class at the Naval Academy. I responded that I had stood 77, which I, privately, considered pretty decent out of a starting class of 1250. But he did not seem to be at all impressed. His questions were, "Did you really try as hard as you could?" "Did you ever go to hops or play sports?" I responded that I had indeed had dates at the dance hops and did play company basketball and softball.

He then said, "You could have stood higher in your class if you hadn't wasted so much time." He gave that a moment to sink in before asking, "Would you do it differently if you had it to do over again?"

His motive for that question may have been to find out if I would learn from experience and do things differently. Or it may have been to see if I harbored self-doubts about past performance. At any rate I simply replied, "No." To which he responded, "I don't think we need a playboy like you around here." He then rambled on about the Naval Academy doing a lousy job of education and that all USNA graduates were basically just spoiled ignoramuses.

Next he asked about what I had done in the Navy so far. I mentioned the various boats I had served on and my tour at MIT He then wanted to know who were the Captains on my submarines. When I mentioned Dennis Wilkinson on the Volador, he asked if I thought Dennis would recommend me for the job I was applying for. When I said yes, he again called his secretary in and said, "Get Commander Wilkinson on the phone." Then back to me, "Does that worry you?" I was getting used to the routine and simply said, "No."

After receiving a positive response from Dennis Wilkinson he concluded the interview by saying that Naval Officers were a spoiled lot and that he wasn't sure I would be any good working in his group. "What do you have to say about that?" he asked.

I answered "Captain Rickover, if I am not selected for this work it won't be the end of the world."

I walked out of his office feeling that he did not like me. My prospects for joining the nuclear submarine program seemed pretty slim. Two weeks later, I received notification that I was one of four selected to go to MIT for the Advanced Nuclear Engineering course. I would report to MIT on June 8, 1953. My classmate, Sam Bassett, was also one of the four selected. Sam and I became good friends and were thesis partners for our Masters Thesis in Nuclear Engineering. The other two were Bill Humphrey, '43, and Dan Brooks, '44.

After selection, to get ready for M.I.T, I was put on a study course by Rickover's office while I was still attached to the K-1. With Cdr. Ed Kintner as my coach I worked through a calculus book and several physics books. Ed also kept me informed on the Nautilus prototype. He notified me of the day March 30, 1953 that the Nautilus prototype first went critical, the day April 30, 1953 that it went to power and the day June 25, 1953 that it went to full power and ran at full power for 100 hours. Rickover loved 100-hour full power runs because he felt they proved the reliability of the Nuclear power plant.

I was mid way through the Masters program at MIT when the Nautilus was officially launched on January 21, 1954. Because of my prior association with the Electric Boat people during construction of the K-1, I was invited for the ceremony. So Mary and I went down from Boston to New London to watch Mamie Eisenhower christen the Nautilus. Later that evening we attended the party at the Officers Club of the Sub Base.

A year later on January 17, 1955, I would be working at NRB when the Nautilus was "underway on Nuclear Power". And in another year I would be the Project Officer for Nautilus and make the plans, budgets, work lists, etc. for the first refueling of the Nautilus from October 1956 to January 1957. After refueling, I rode Nautilus on Final Acceptance trials the 14th and 15th of January 1957. The two years between Initial Trials and Final Acceptance trials were spent changing and fixing items to be able to pass the Final Acceptance trials. I was Project Officer during two thirds of that period.

I completed the Masters of Science, Nuclear Engineering on July 22, 1954, with an overall GPA of 4.79 on a 5.0 scale. There were thirteen courses covering such areas as Nuclear

Figure 60   USS Triton (SSRN 586) Two Engine Room Nuclear Submarine. Captain Ned Beach made trip around the world submerged.

Physics, Advanced Calculus for Engineers and Nuclear Reactor Engineering. My thesis was on neutron flux flattening by using non-uniform fuel distribution and burnable poisons in power reactors. Before reporting to Bureau of Ships, Nuclear Propulsion Division and Naval Reactor Branch, Atomic Energy Commission in Washington DC, Rickover had me visit Nuclear Power Plants in Savannah Georgia, Hanford Washington, Naval Reactor Test Station in Arco Idaho, Argonne National Lab, Brookhaven National lab, the GE Knolls Atomic Power Lab in Schenectady NY and the Westinghouse Bettis Lab in Pittsburgh.

In August, 1954 I reported in to Rickover's staff. I was first assigned to the Advanced Development Group. My immediate boss was my former coach, Cdr. Ed Kintner who did not like nuts and bolts engineering work and therefore was put into the dream world of new ideas where he did not have problems with final design and construction work. My job was to work on system designs and compartment arrangements for a one reactor, two-engine room steam plant. This Radar Picket Submarine Project was eventually called the USS Triton (SSRN586).

The assignment was a bit of a coincidence since my first submarine assignment in 1946 after graduation from Submarine School was aboard the USS Grouper (SS214), an old fleet boat that had been fitted out to be a radar picket submarine. The Chief's quarters had been gutted and PPI (Plan Position Indicator) scopes had been installed in addition to VHF equipment, plotting boards and other paraphernalia of a small CIC (Combat Information Center). From this installation we could conduct intercepts of incoming bogeys and vector our planes to engage the "enemy planes". The overall concept of this submarine was to perform picket duty and if attacked by enemy aircraft the submarine picket could submerge until the attacking aircraft left or was downed by "friendlies".

Rickover had the idea of FBM (Fleet Ballistic Missile) submarines and believed that for that purpose we would need a two engine room, two turbine steam plant, driving two propellers on a large submarine. He wanted to build a large submarine that could perform this function. But there was not an operational requirement for such a submarine because we did not have a missile for such a ship. Grasping at straws, Rickover pushed CNO's Ships Characteristic Board to say they needed a Radar Picket Submarine that was fast enough to stay ahead of a carrier task force and thus needed lots of power to make 30 knots and hold position ahead of the task force. Thus we designed and built the only two engine room nuclear submarine.

With Dave Leighton as Project Officer, I was made Technical Manager of the SAR (Submarine Advanced Reactor) Project, later called the S3G Project. My title was changed to Head of Advanced Submarine Projects. I was on this job until the ship characteristics had been set - tonnage, speed, power, etc. - and preliminary plans were complete and the ship construction could go out for bid.

At 412 feet the Triton was the longest sub that could be built in the ways at Electric Boat. I know this for a fact because we had to lengthen the Triton three times in the planning stage in order to have enough buoyancy to compensate for the weight of the power plant. The bow was touching the overhead railway and the stern was in the water. We had reached the maximum length possible.

The Triton Prototype (S3G) was built at West Milton, New York. The Triton was launched in August 1958 and it was commissioned and went to sea in 1959. It was the first submarine to circumnavigate the globe submerged. In 1960 Captain Beach accomplished this mission in 83 days.

The Tullibee Project was started toward the end of the time I was Head of Advanced Submarine Projects. The Admiral had as one of the objectives of this project to get a third reactor design and construction group in the nuclear business. Since the start of NRB, General Electric and Westinghouse were the only reactor contractors.

Rickover drove a hard bargain and convinced Combustion Engineering to pay for about half of the test facility needed to do the work on the Tullibee Project. If I remember right, the cost to Combustion was over ten million dollars. Around July 1955, Rickover had me arrange a program for a team of ten of our people to make a background presentation to all the engineers at Combustion. We put on an all day program covering the subjects of Reactor Design, Plant Layout, System Design, Shielding Design, Reactor Control, Thermal Stress Studies, Turbine Characteristics and Noise Reduction. I gave the talks on Plant Layout, System Design and Noise Reduction.

The requirements for the Tullibee came about because submarine officers, especially Captain Dick Lanning, believed that many small submarines would be better than a few large submarines such as Nautilus. CNO had asked the Ship Characteristics Board to write up the characteristics desired for a small hunter-killer submarine powered by a nuclear reactor.

I believe the proposal was for a 2000 ton, 15 knot quiet submarine. The Admiral asked me to work up estimates of the power plant needed for such a boat and to make some rough estimates of costs.

My engineers and one naval architect concluded that such a boat with a nuclear reactor and steam plant would have to displace at least 3000 tons and cost would be about $35 million. We had Nautilus (S2W) and Skate (S5W) designs from which to make extrapolations. We had prepared other studies of size, speed and tonnage and we could be fairly accurate as to ballpark figures.

When I took the study to the Admiral, he went into a rage screaming, "Callahan, you must be the dumbest officer in the whole US Navy."

I replied, as calmly as possible, "Admiral, I didn't come in to talk about me. I came in to discuss the results of the Tullibee study."

The Admiral proceeded to tell me that my numbers were all wrong, the conclusions as to the tonnage and costs were ridiculous and he would get someone else to make the study. So Edson Case became Project Officer for Tullibee.

The Admiral had told some of his friends in Congress that he could build a small, nuclear powered submarine for $20 million. He had not told me this. He could not accept the results I gave him because he could not get approval for a small submarine that cost $35 million.

The procedure was to tell Congress you could do the project for what they were willing to pay. After the Project is approved, you go back each year and say the cost has gone up until you get enough money to do the job. This type of estimating is what causes all the cost overruns in Defense Department projects. I was just not willing to lie and provide impossible estimates.

By the way, the Tullibee ended up at 3100 tons and cost over $40,000,000 to build.

After finishing Triton and Tullibee studies I moved from Head of Advanced Submarine Projects to Project Officer of the Nautilus and Seawolf. With the Nautilus and Seawolf I also took over responsibility for the Nautilus Prototype at the Naval Reactor Test Station in Utah and the Seawolf Prototype at West Milton, NY. This meant I had responsibility to the Admiral for all of the operating plants since nothing else was built at the time. Needless to say, I had constant meetings with Admiral Rickover because operating plants have more problems than plants in design on paper. I began to understand the Rickover system. When I first became head technical man for the Triton and later the Tullibee, I would request permission to see the Admiral and ask him to approve decisions that needed to be made. Even though I was well prepared for the encounter, it would always end up in a screaming session and no decision. I guess maybe in the hollering session, Admiral Rickover would suggest I write down what I was recommending as obviously I could not adequately express my thought orally.

It finally dawned on me that Admiral Rickover was a political animal. What he really wanted were recommendations in writing so when a problem would surface, he could haul out a memo and say "Here was USNA graduate, top 5%, two advanced degrees from MIT, 7 years as a submarine officer and he made this recommendation. I can't do everything myself and as soon as I found out he caused this problem, I fired him." Once I realized he was just a politician trying to cover his own rear and not the technical genius he pushed his PR to claim, I knew how to get my job done.

All I had to do was sign an official memorandum from F. J. Callahan to H.G. Rickover and I could get quick approval for anything that I considered necessary to do. I realized that he was covering his political position. Once I came to this conclusion, I was able to run my programs on Nautilus and Seawolf without major fights, knowing that if anything went wrong, I was the fall guy.

This was Rickover's undeclared method of delegating authority. It is also the typical modus operandi for bureaucrats in general.

One iron clad rule in Rickover's operation was that letters, memos and rough drafts that were typed on any typewriter anyplace in his organization were to have a pink carbon copy. These were collected daily, put in a folder and presented to Rickover in the morning so that he could read anything that entered a typewriter the preceding day. In this manner, he was checking everyone and looking over their preliminary work on a continuing basis.

A continuous stream of people would be called to Rickover's office to be challenged on the content of their "pinks". Many people used the "pinks" as a sounding board with Rickover by having rough drafts of letters or reports typed by their secretaries and then wait for a call to defend their work. In order to avoid confrontations on matters that I had not thought through or had

Figure 61   USS Nautilus (SSN 571) First Nuclear Powered Submarine.
It was Captained by my ex-skipper, Dennis P. Wilkinson.

not discussed with other department heads, I wrote everything out in long hand until I was ready to go to press and defend my position. I did not have rough drafts typed. I waited until I had a smooth copy ready for signature before I turned it over for typing. In this manner, I presented letters for Rickover's signature before he had a chance to read a pink. I don't know if this did me any good, but at least I didn't have to defend rough drafts and semi-finished work that I was not ready to hang my hat on.

It might seem that this system could be avoided by just having your secretary not put in a pink on certain work. But from the first day a secretary was hired the head of administration made it very clear that any secretary who did not put a pink in any time the typewriter was used, would be fired on the first offense.

The inefficiencies of this system were that dictation was seldom used and a lot of hand written drafts were made in order to avoid confrontation with Admiral Rickover.

While I was Project Officer for the Nautilus, Rickover asked me to write a paper on the problems a submarine would have making a transit under the ice. In preparation I read several reports on "blue nose" cruises, the descriptive name for cruises in the Arctic made by diesel submarines. These boats tested out underwater sonar for detecting ice above and ahead. There was also much information on brash ice and percent coverage of solid ice that would be encountered in an under the pole transit.

It appeared to me that early fall when ice coverage was minimal would be the best time to attempt such a transit and of course the symbolic surfacing at the pole. Inertial navigation had improved so that navigation was not as difficult as it had been earlier. (When you are at the pole, all directions are south.)

Nuclear boats could stay submerged indefinitely because

they had small chemical plants that removed the CO and CO2 from the air. Length of submergence in itself was not a problem. I felt the major danger was fire while submerged which would rapidly deplete oxygen and make breathing impossible due to smoke and poisonous gases. Our usual procedure with fires while submerged was to isolate the fire, surface the boat and ventilate unaffected compartments. A boat under the ice could not surface until it was in open areas of brash ice or below relatively thin ice. I recommended extensive fire drills and carrying of extra oxygen breathing equipment to handle potential fire problems.

Once I turned in my recommendations, I do not know whether anyone ever paid attention to them or not. I never had a comment from Rickover on my study or did he ever mention it after I turned it in. It must have been pretty good because he never passed up a chance to raise hell with any report he did not think was perfect.

I think it was around January 1956 that I had another revealing run in with Admiral Rickover. I was Project Officer for Nautilus.

The Nautilus came in from sea on Friday. The Captain reported that they might have some vibration in the starboard turbine. He thought it would be a good idea to have personnel from the turbine manufacturer come out the following week with special instruments to determine if a problem existed and asked me to authorize the test. I contacted the manufacturer and made arrangements for them to run a check on Monday morning and report the results to me.

Early Monday afternoon, I was summoned by Rickover. "Callahan, get down to my office right now!" When I was ushered into his office I was greeted with, "Callahan, who the hell do you think you are?"

Calmly, because I had been through the drill before, "Lt. Callahan, United States Navy, Admiral."

"Don't get smart with me Callahan. Who in the hell gave you the right to determine if there was a turbine problem on the Nautilus? Don't you know that if something is wrong with the Nautilus it is extremely important and that I should have been advised?"

"Admiral, if there was something wrong, I would have advised you. If I told you there might be something wrong, you would have raised as much hell as you are right now for telling you that something might be wrong. Why would I waste your time telling you something might be wrong?"

"Callahan this job is just too damn big for you. I ought to replace you with someone else."

"Admiral, if you can find someone else to take this job, just tell me and I'm out of here." With that I left.

For two weeks after that, Admiral Rickover followed the most unusual behavior. He was very nice to me. Almost unheard of for anyone who worked for him. I figured he knew that I had had it up to my Navy ribbons and would leave with no regrets. Then he would have to break in someone else who would listen to his screaming for two years.

I concluded from this that he really didn't want me to report on things that might be a problem. Almost anything might be a problem. If I kept telling him what might be problems, he would really be justified in telling me that the job was too big for me. What he really wanted was to be on record as having demanded to be informed. That way if anyone ever accused him of not knowing something, he could say that he had repeatedly demanded to be informed of even the smallest detail by his subordinates.

We had a standing method of operation that worked on the premise that if you told him ten things, you got chewed out ten times. But if you got caught not telling him one of those ten things you only got chewed out once.

Prior to one of the Nautilus upkeeps, the Nautilus Chief Engineer had recommended that a one-inch in diameter piece of pipe that was six inches long be cut off the main coolant piping. The pipe stub served no purpose and was actually a hindrance. It was attached to the bottom of the main coolant pipe and extended downward. In this position, it had collected "crud" - the name for corrosion products from the stainless steel used in the primary loop. This "crud" was radioactive and the six-inch stub was the highest source of radioactive activity in the lower reactor compartment. In order to work for any length of time in the lower reactor compartment, it was necessary to take lead bricks down and shield off this source of radioactivity before work could be started. The fact that it was a strong source of radioactivity was the main reason the ship's personnel wanted the stub removed.

Dennis Wilkinson, the Commanding Officer of Nautilus strongly agreed with this request as did all technical personnel from Bettis, Electric Boats, SupShips and Naval Reactors Branch. To all concerned this was such a no brainer and such a minor job that I concurred and told them to go ahead and cut it off.

After it had been successfully removed and a plug welded in to fill the boss, Wilkinson inadvertently mentioned to the Admiral how great it was to have gotten rid of this nuisance. Then the shit hit the fan.

Lt. Callahan was summoned to Admiral Rickover's office.

"Callahan, who the hell do you think you are? Who ever gave you the right to make ship alterations? Do you think you can take over my job?"

"What's wrong now, Admiral?"

"Do you think you have authority to change the Primary Coolant System on Nautilus without getting my permission?"

"No sir. I haven't changed the Primary Coolant System. What is this outburst about?"

"Didn't you OK the removal of a piece of pipe from the reactor system on the Nautilus?"

"For God's Sake, Admiral, it was only a 6" stub of pipe that was a bad radiation source. There was absolutely no function it performed and everyone wanted to get rid of the radiation source to make it easier to get work done in the lower level."

"You call them right now and tell them to put that piece of pipe back in. I expect it to be done before they go back to sea."

"Admiral that's ridiculous. Even if I did exceed my authority, now that it is out it is stupid to put it back in."

"Are you calling me stupid? You call them right now or I'll do it myself."

"It's a mistake, but Aye Aye Sir."

The ship's company forever blamed me for the fact that the pipe stub again became the worse source of radiation in the lower reactor compartment of Nautilus.

This was the only time I gave in to the Admiral when I knew I was right. I should have let him make the call to have the six inch pipe put back in. I regret that I didn't stand my ground.

When we were finally approaching initial trials on Seawolf, Admiral Rickover decided that as a reward for all their hard work, about 25 of the NRB personnel should go to sea on the first operation of the Sodium Reactor Powered Sea Wolf. He sent this list to Carl Shugg, the President of Electric Boat Division of General Dynamics.

Shortly after this list was sent, I received frantic calls from three sources. Carl Shugg called protesting impracticality of have 25 NRB personnel on board. Calls also came from Commander Willie Shor and Captain Chet Smith the US Navy Supervisor for Shipbuilding at Electric Boat. All were in complete agreement that taking this many people out on initial trials would be a circus. They basically said that if NRB wanted

***Figure 62   USS Seawolf (SSN 575)   Only Nuclear Submarine
with a Sodium Cooled Reactor.***

to take all these people out to make them feel good, we could go out for a few hours and then bring them back in. We would then run the sea trials after they were taken ashore.

For a period of two weeks, almost on a daily basis I made the case for why it was impractical to take such a large contingent on the initial trials. I used various arguments. Each was met with the usual put downs for which Rickover was famous. At no time was there even the slightest indication that he would change his mind.

The day before we were to go out on trials, I received a call from Shugg asking me how I got things changed. I said I didn't know what he was talking about. He said, "I just got a call from Admiral Rickover. He now says that he will be accompanied by Ted Rockwell and Joe Callahan. That the three of you will be the only NRB personnel to ride on the Seawolf trials."

After the Seawolf with a sodium-cooled reactor successfully finished initial trials, it was obvious that the Nautilus, with a pressurized water plant, had a far better power plant for the sea environment.

Sodium and water do not get along very well when mixed, explosion and fire being one result. If it was the only way we could have had a true submersible operating under the water at high power without consuming oxygen, the sodium plant would have been acceptable. However, the success of the Pressurized Water Reactor (PWR) on the Nautilus, made it unnecessary to continue development of the sodium plant which still had many problems.

It was not publicized, but the Sodium plant on the Seawolf had a very successful history of operation. The Seawolf operated for one year after initial sea trials without a problem that required entry into the reactor compartment for repair. On the other hand, the Nautilus reactor compartment was entered into many times for minor repairs.

Why then the decision to recommend the replacement of the Seawolf Sodium cooled reactor with a Pressurized Water Reactor? The first and overriding problem was that the radiation levels in the Seawolf reactor compartment were so high, with a relatively long half-life that in event of a casualty, you could not enter the reactor compartment for over two weeks. By contrast in the Nautilus, after the 15 to 30 minutes needed to remove the lead shielding plugs from the deck in order to enter the compartment, the radiation was already down to a level that emergency repairs could be carried out. A two week wait to even begin repairs seemed intolerable to submariners who had been depth charged in WW II and had to take rapid damage control measures in order to save their boats.

Of equal importance to the practicality of a Sodium cooled plant was a problem that was never solved in the design of the plant. If the reactor plant cooled down and the sodium solidified, there was no routine for being able to re-liquefy the sodium and put the plant back in operation. The optimist might say that since the plant operated for a year and had no such problem that it would probably never happen. However, a simple fire in the electrical panel that kept the calrods hot and the sodium liquefied when the reactor was not running, could disable the plant forever. Or another scenario, a fire of the calrod control panel would cause shutdown of the reactor and with no power to the calrods, the sodium would solidify and the plant could not be restarted. You don't build multi-million dollar ships that can be ruined by the failure of one electrical panel.

This was basically the thrust of the report that I prepared, with comments from other department heads of the Naval

Reactor Branch. The report was submitted to Congress requesting funds for the replacement of the Sodium Plant on Seawolf with a PWR (Pressurized Water Reactor Plant).

To forward this report to Congress, I prepared a letter for CNO's signature that summarized these conclusions and requested funding for the replacement. When I presented this two-page letter to Admiral Rickover, he read through it and finding nothing wrong, he proceeded to the sign-off page and initialed his large "R".

Then he screamed, "Callahan, I can never trust you to do a complete job." With that he threw his fountain pen onto the top page scattering ink all over it.

I couldn't imagine what was wrong. Since he had no complaint while reading the letter, this took me back a bit. I said, "Admiral, what is wrong?"

He proceeded to show me that my secretary had failed to enter the date under his sign-off square on the yellow copy page. This could easily have been added, but his messing up the front page meant my secretary had to re-type the whole letter. (This was of course prior to word processors.) I said, "Thank you Admiral, you have just made a lot of unnecessary work for my secretary."

As I was leaving the room, Dave Leighton was standing outside the door. He had obviously witnessed the screaming and I gave him an embarrassed smile. I had not gone more than five steps, when Admiral Rickover came running after me saying, "Callahan, what is so funny about all this? This is important Defense Department business and is nothing to laugh about." He had seen me smile to Leighton in his glass front bookcases as I was leaving his room.

Turning around I said, "Admiral, what do you want me to do? Cry."

He treated me nice for a week because he knew I had reached the point of leaving again. And indeed I had. In August of 1957 I submitted my resignation from the Navy. Rickover endorsed it with the provision that I be retained for four months so I could be properly relieved. Rick Claytor was assigned to relieve me.

In November 1957 Nautilus, while in port, took in about 6 feet of seawater into the lower level of the reactor compartment. I don't remember the details concerning which valve was left open, but it was not in the lower level of the reactor compartment because there were no sea valves in the lower level. The sea water got into the trenches where the steam risers came through the deck and the flexible joints that allowed for thermal expansion of the risers failed which allowed the sea water to enter the lower reactor compartment.

Once discovered, it was not a great problem to cut off the source of the seawater and pump it out. However the possibilities of chloride stress corrosion cracking of the stainless steel piping and other stainless steel components of the primary system endangered the safety of the reactor plant. The only solution was that the primary system had to be washed with distilled water until no chlorides remained. To do this all the insulation had to be removed first.

At this time, ComSubLand (I think it was Admiral Freddie Warder) was attempting to assume responsibility for the upkeep and repair of Nautilus since it was a Navy ship assigned to his command. He had sent the ship to Electric Boat Company and Captain Smith, the Supervisor of Shipbuilding and SubLant's Chief Engineer were trying to reach a decision on the necessary action. Admiral Rickover considered the Nautilus his responsibility and refused to offer advice or allow anyone from Naval Reactor Branch to get involved unless ComSubLant would relinquish responsibility and ask him to take charge of the upkeep and repair of USS Nautilus and other nuclear submarines in the future.

There was about a four-day stalemate and ComSubLant and Electric Boats management had come to the conclusion that the Nautilus needed to be dry- docked, the hull cut open and components removed from the primary system. This would have taken six to eight months when you take into account all the testing needed to bring the reactor plant back on line. At this point, Admiral Warder asked Rickover for help and relinquished repair of the Nautilus to Rickover.

Rickover called me on a Saturday morning and told me to

Figure 63   Rickover inspects the Nautilus.

go to New London to investigate the flooding. He gave me a list of questions to ask in order to fix the responsibility for the flooding. He then asked me what my objectives were when I got to New London. I told him that I intended to try to avoid the dry-docking, opening of the hull and cutting into the primary system. For the first time in three and one-half years, he actually seemed to respect my objective and asked, "Do you really think there is a chance that cleaning can be done without dry-docking and cutting into the pressure hull?"

I said, "Admiral, I don't know, but I am going to make every effort to get that system cleaned up without cutting into the ship and the primary system."

Rick Claytor and I left before noon and arrived at Electric Boats about 3:00 PM. We were ushered into a conference room with about twenty people, including Carl Shugg and Captain Smith. They had the ship and docking plans laid out and started to discuss the plans for the job. I stopped the presentation and asked, "Why can't we get the insulation off the system and wash it down in place"

They answered that the laggers who had put in the insulation and work supervisors who had checked the area said there was not room enough to get the insulation out without opening the hull and also removing the main coolant pumps from the primary system. I decided we would give it a try. I said "Let's get the workmen started on taking the salt water soaked insulation off. When they can't get anymore off, have them call me. I will sleep on the work barge and they can wake me up any time during the night. If they reach a point they can't get any more insulation off then we will discuss docking and other plans."

When I awoke at 8:00 AM, I went over to the Nautilus and asked the supervisor how things were going. He told me that all of the insulation had been removed and that we could start working on procedures for cleaning up the primary system.

Rick Claytor asked me how I knew that the insulation could be taken off. Of course I didn't know for sure. But I knew for sure it was worth a try. I remembered the coils on the main motors of the K-1 that supposedly couldn't be removed. This was the same problem but on a bigger scale.

I figure I saved the Navy over $3 million dollars by forcing the attempt to remove the insulation. This paid for all the education that the Navy had given me over my years in the Navy. Also, my performance on this job is probably the reason Rickover offered me a Civil Service rating of GS18 if I would stay and work for him as a civilian. My response was, "I am a Naval Officer, not a Civil Servant".

If I had wanted to stay in, it would have been as a Naval Officer, not a bureaucrat.

As a postscript on Rickover, it did not take as much nerve as you might think to be sassy with the Admiral. For one thing I understood that his hollering was just a way to find out if his staff had the courage to stand up to Presidents and Vice Presidents at General Electric, Electric Boat and Westinghouse. And two, the job was very stressful. Getting fired would have been the best thing that could happen. It would be like going on a permanent vacation.

6

It is better to finish one job than to start one hundred.

Naval Career - Naval Reserves

My resignation from the Regular Navy (USN) became effective with my discharge on January 6, 1958. The same day, I accepted membership in the United States Naval Reserve (USNR) as Lieutenant commander (LCDR, USNR).

About a week after arriving at Kenmore Research Company in Framingham, Massachusetts as Managing Director, I joined the Naval Reserve Research Company in Worcester, which was just down the highway. I considered joining the Naval Research Company at MIT, which was also an option. But there were several hundred officers at MIT compared to about a dozen at Worcester University. I preferred the smaller unit.

In October 1958, we moved to Chagrin Falls, Ohio to take a job at Nupro Company. I became a member of Naval Reserve Research Company 4-8, which operated out of the Naval Reserve Center at the corner of 9th Street and the Shoreway in downtown Cleveland. I remained a member of 4-8 until 1973 when the rapid increase in growth of our companies demanded more of my time. I became inactive in the reserve until retiring in 1983, completing 41 years of association with the Navy.

Captain Vicktor Shreckingost, a noted artist in Cleveland, was the Commanding Officer of Naval Reserve Research Company 4-8 when I came on board in 1958. In about 1961 Vicktor retired from the Naval Reserve and I became commanding Officer of the Company.

While a member of the Navy Reserve, it was necessary to meet certain requirements to be retained in the Active Reserve. One was the requirement to attend, in uniform, meetings at 6:00 PM on two Mondays every month.

At the Monday evening meetings we had lectures on many technical subjects. Or we made field trips to a business or facility that would be of technical interest. As a result, we visited NASA, the Regional Air Control Center at Oberlin, the new Tertiary Sewage Plant for Cleveland, Cleveland Clinic Foundation and all sorts of manufacturing plants, steel mills and research labs. We stuck our noses in everybody's business.

One example of our Monday evening meetings was a field trip to Walker China, which was located on Solon Road in Northfield. An officer in our Navy Reserve Research Company was a ceramic engineer who worked at Walker China. On his invitation we made a tour of the plant.

Before we started the tour we were given an introduction

talk about Walker China in a conference room. Examples of their products such as the gilt edged plates at the Union Club and plates from many of the private clubs in Cleveland where shown to us. They also explained to us that foreign companies were able to produce china at a much lower cost and their business was going downhill.

When we toured the plant we saw how the gilt edge was put on a dinner plate. The plate was placed on a rotating wooden spindle and the operator tapped the plate until it was centered on the spindle. He then dipped a small paint brush in the gilt paint and held the brush by hand on the edge of the plate, applying a band about 3/16" wide to the edge of the plate as it rotated. He then waited about three minutes for the paint to dry before he removed the plate and started the cycle over again.

At another location was a woman sitting in the center of four stacks of plates, each stack had a different size plate. The stacks were about five feet high. She took a plate from the top of the stack and placed it in front of her. She then took a rubber stamp that had "Walker China, Cleveland, Ohio" on it, hit the inkpad with the stamp and then stamped the back of the plate. I told them that we stamped boxes and other items in a similar manner at my plant. I related our experience to indicate a better way. We had the rubber stamp operated by a foot pedal to stamp the surface and when released, it automatically was pressed against the inkpad. In this manner you picked up the part to be stamped, positioned the part, hit the foot pedal to stamp it and put the part down. They said that this wouldn't work for them because the stamps were of different sizes for different plates, even though they had plates of the same size stacked to the ceiling waiting to be stamped. I decided that Walker China was making plates under medieval conditions and would probably go broke.

In addition to the two Monday a month meetings, I also had

Figure 64   Official photo after making Captain, July 1, 1966.

to complete a correspondence course commensurate with my grade and go on active duty for two weeks every year. As my rank got higher, the correspondence course became more time consuming. The courses I took while in the rank of Captain were to prepare me to become an Admiral in the Naval Reserve. Each course I took while Captain was equivalent to a thesis once a year. I did graduate from the Naval War College by correspondence course and was in line for promotion to Admiral when I decided that my business and civic demands and my budding golf-aholic tendencies did not leave me time to spend another five years to make Admiral USNR. So I quit going on active duty and doing correspondence courses in

1972. I retired from the Naval Reserves as a Captain on my 60th birthday in 1983.

On the following pages I will relate some of my experiences in the two-week active duty service I had in the Naval Reserves. These active duty tours were fun and productive because I could spend two weeks with no other duty except studying a problem. With no telephone to answer and no staff to manage, it is amazing how much can be accomplished in a short time. It also helped that all the people I approached for information about a problem knew that I had the blessings of the Admiral for the project.

Naval Reserve Research Company at Oak Ridge

In November 1959, I attended a two-week seminar put on by the Naval Reserve Research Company at Oak Ridge Tennessee on Uranium Enrichment, Nuclear Reactors and Nuclear Health Physics. At the time, Oak Ridge was one of Swagelok's largest customers and this gave me two weeks to meet a lot of our customers, see our distributor and review what was going on at Oak Ridge National Lab.

I had been to Oak Ridge several times while working for Rickover so it was a very familiar place to be for my first Naval Reserve Active Duty.

ONR Seminar - Washington DC

In June 1960 I attended the Office of Naval Research Seminar in Washington on government patent policy and a series of major research programs being funded by ONR. One of these programs the LOFAR system, consisted of very long cable arrays on the ocean floor where low frequency sounds were heard at great distances. I never talked about this system because I considered it "secret". Later I read a complete description of the system in *Hunt for Red October* by Tom Clancy, so I guess I can now mention it.

I still had a lot of friends in the Washington area from my days on Rickover's staff and enjoyed visiting with them. Rickover was out of the country at that time so I did not have to make the decision of whether to try seeing him or not.

Bureau of Ships Code 500 - USS Thresher (SSN593)

For my active duty assignment in 1962 I requested and received orders to Code 500, the Submarine Desk of the Bureau of Ships. On my second day there, reports were received from Thresher that six or seven brazed joints had failed during depth charge exercises off Key West. These depth charge exercises consisted of a destroyer running parallel to the submarine at about 100 yards and dropping depth charges so submarine crews would know what depth charges felt and sounded like when close at hand. The submarine ran at periscope depth, with periscopes up so there would be no accidental "hits". I had experienced this type of exercise while on USS Volador.

I asked Commander Kern how many brazed joints were being used on the boats. He told me that many monel sea lines, up to 8 inches in diameter, were being brazed instead of welded. I told him that while I had been at Naval Reactor Branch (Code 1500, Bureau of Ships) I had not allowed lines that were to be at full sea pressure to be brazed if they were over one inch in diameter. He said that in WWII the fleet boats had six inch lines in the engine room that were brazed and that there were no reported failures. I replied that these lines were for running the diesel engine and were only open while on the surface. The sea valves were shut upon diving so they never saw pressure at full submergence. I asserted that all the lines on the Thresher should have been welded.

As a result of this discussion I was given the job of determining the size line failure the submarine's main blow system should be designed to handle. I was surprised when I started to look into this problem to find that the air system on Thresher was the same as on the old fleet boats. Since Thresher displaced two and one-half times as much as a fleet boat and could go almost three times deeper, it certainly seemed that more consideration should have been given to a much higher capacity air blow system. As a result of having the same air system there was a major discrepancy in the amount of time needed on Thresher to blow ballast than on a fleet boat. I concluded a fleet boat could blow about ten times more effectively than Thresher at test depth. Even with all air banks on the line, Thresher could not displace the same percent of displacement a fleet boat could. I concluded that it took 27 times as long to blow 1% of the displacement on Thresher as it did a Fleet boat.

The math is fairly simple. Assume an air bank has 60 cubic feet at 3000 pounds pressure on the surface. It was standard procedure on submarines, including Thresher, to have two air banks on the line when submerged. That gives 120 cubic feet on the line. Here's a quick calculation to show the difference in the maximum water blown in a fleet boat that goes to 400 feet versus a boat such as Thresher that goes to 1200 feet.

At a depth of 400 feet the sea pressure is 178 pounds per square inch. So the volume of air in our two tanks becomes 3000 divided by 178 (which is 16.85) times 120 cubic feet giving us 2022 cubic feet of air. Subtracting the cubic feet of tanks we were able to blow out about 1902 cubic feet of water. Since sea water weights 64 pounds per cubic foot we could lighten the boat by 61 tons.

Following the same calculations at 1200 feet with a sea pressure of 532 pounds per square inch, we could only blow out 18 tons of water.

So the Thresher could only blow 18 tons to 61 tons for a fleet boat. The discrepancy is even more significant when looked at as a percentage of displacement. The 4100 ton Thresher was able to displace only 0.4% of its total mass. (18 divided by 4100). However the 1500 ton fleet boats were able to displace 4% of their mass. (61 divided by 1500).

Based on my analysis I made the following recommendations:

1. That Commanding Officers of Thresher Class submarines should be advised to carry all air banks on the line as part of rig for dive.

2. That ship's characteristics should carry a requirement to blow a certain percentage of total displacement within a given length of time. (This would make it necessary to review this system design for every new submarine design.)

3. That valves from the air bank should be installed to blow directly into the tanks in which they were stored so that the air did not have to go through the control room manifold. Line losses caused the blowing time to be much too slow for deep diving boats.

4. That all brazed connections over 1" should be welded.

I argued that the size of the casualty was not what should be considered. The main ballast tank blow system should be looked at as a ship control system. At times when we blew main ballast to stop descent past 400 feet in a Fleet Boat, it seemed to take forever to stop the momentum. On Thresher it took ten times forever.

Submarine Development Group II

In December 1962 I submitted a request for active duty for the following year with SubDevGruII in New London. My skipper from the K-1, Captain Frank Andrews, was Commander of Submarine Development Group II at the time and, since we were good friends, I thought two weeks there would be time well spent. Our days on the K-1 were also under the command of ComSubDevGruII.

On April 10, 1963 the nuclear submarine, USS Thresher (SSN-593), with 16 officers, 96 enlisted men and 17 civilian technicians was lost at sea. That morning the ship was off the coast of New England with the USS Skylark. The two ships were in communication by means of underwater sound telephone. At 7:47 AM the Thresher started a deep dive. At 9:13 AM Thresher sent the message: "We are experiencing minor difficulties, we have a positive up angle and are attempting to blow. Will keep you informed." Skylark received two more garbled messages before detecting a high energy, low frequency disturbance, the crushing of Thresher as she dropped below her crush depth.

The Thresher had been located by magnetic search and the Trieste was enroute to the scene. Frank Andrews was scheduled to go to Portsmouth, New Hampshire and go down in the Trieste to study the debris. He asked if I wanted to go along. I responded that of course I wanted to go but didn't think as a reservist I should take the place of a regular officer on such important work. I then asked Frank if BuShips had sent him a copy of my recommendations as to how the blow system should be rigged. He said he had never heard of it, but he would request a copy.

During the investigation of the Thresher accident, I was told that my report from my active duty assignment in 1962 had come up. It was said that I had predicted the loss of Thresher. This is not true. I had merely pointed out the danger of brazed joints and the inadequacy of the blow system. At no time did I predict that the Thresher would be lost.

When I reported aboard in June, I found my classmate, Jim Bellas, busy handling affairs of the surviving family members of the crew. I also ran into an Engineering Duty Officer (EDO) from BuShips and asked him why they used the brazed joints after all the time I had spent arguing against them. He said that lab tests proved that brazed joints were stronger than welded joints and that they saved $100,000 per submarine by brazing the monel rather than welding it.

Brazed joints are theoretically stronger because the base metal is not annealed. However, the difficulty of making large size braze joints made them unreliable. To make this braze, you must heat up the joint and the gap between the male and female member must be .002" to .003" around the circumference for capillary action to carry the brazing material into the joint. In shipboard construction, blow torches were arranged around the joint and distortion took place so flow completely around the joint was unlikely. Besides, at that time there were not good ultrasonic tests to prove that the joint was sound.

A report title "Findings on Thresher" in the March/April 1965 issue of *Ordinance* made the following statements, with which I disagree:

"………*Remember the garbled last message from Thresher about 'trying to blow up…experiencing minor difficulty..'. It was not until after the loss of Thresher that a test was made (this at dockside) to completely blow the high-pressure air for deballasting.*

"Part way through the test the air stopped moving through the pipes. Ice had formed over the screens in the system, blocking them completely. There is a 2-to-1 pressure drop in the system, and ice formed through the simple and well-known phenomenon that causes aircraft (and sometimes automobile) carburetors to ice up. Since that test, these screens have been removed."

It would appear that the "2-to-1" drop mentioned in the article should say 200-to-1 and is probably a misprint. The above conclusion about the freezing of the screens in the blow system is wrong. The tests made along side the dock had a pressure drop from 3000 to 15 pounds per square inch (200 to 1). On the Thresher at test depth it was 3000 to 532 pounds per square inch (sea pressure at 1200') and piping was surrounded by sea water that would keep the screens at near sea water temperature. The decompression from 3000 to 532 psi (5.64 : 1) is much less likely to cause an icing problem than the dockside test from 3000 to 15 psi (200 : 1).

Although loss of the Thresher was uppermost in the minds of the officers of SubGroup Two, I was given the job of evaluating the performance of a homing torpedo which I think was the Mark 43. Over one hundred firings had been made and there appeared to be erratic results because many torpedoes that the firing subs thought should be hits were actually misses. Somehow the homing torpedo did not lock on the target.

In submarine approaches with steam or electric torpedoes it was always desirable to keep the torpedo run down to a minimum range. You had to allow about 300 yards for the torpedo to arm. I took the data from all the firings and plotted the sub and target positions when the torpedo activated or did not activate. It gave a clear picture that the torpedo's sonar search lobe was not picking up the noise from the screws of the surface ship if the firing was made at too close a range with the submarine at shallow depth.

ONR - Brookhaven National Lab

In March 1964 I attended an Office of Naval Research seminar at Brookhaven national Lab on Long Island, New York. The seminar was on new particle accelerators and the use of cloud chambers to find particles smaller than neutrons and protons.

I had applied to go to this seminar because I had read that Sam Goudsmit, the man who theoretically put the spin on electrons in the orbit of an atom, had become the Director of Brookhaven National Laboratory. He had tutored three other Naval officers and me the summer we entered MIT for the Nuclear Engineering Course. He was probably the best teacher I have ever had. If you asked him how long it would take to prove the theory of relativity he would say. "Only five minutes if I start five minutes from the end. But two weeks if I start at the beginning." His description of particle physics and the collisions and interactions were always described with Jaguars and pool balls.

ONR - Code 466

Since I was in the Research Reserve, I was being supported by Office of Naval Research. They preferred that I take active duty with them. So for two weeks active duty in1965 I was assigned to Code 466 in Washington. Code 466 had responsibility for deep diving submarines, specifically the "Alvin".

The Alvin was a sphere made to look like a small submarine about 20 feet long that could go to 8000 feet. It had cameras, lights, claws for retrieval and two small battery powered

Figure 65   The Alvin.

propellers for propulsion. The battery's capacity did not perform as well as specified and I was given the job to find out why. This resulted in a 14 page report analyzing the problem and possible solutions. I remember that the main problem was that they had used truck batteries instead of golf cart batteries. Truck batteries operate at the top of the cycle, that is always close to fully charged. Golf cart batteries are subjected to deep discharge. Alvin needed the deep discharge battery to get longer submerged time.

Office of Chief of Naval Operations (OP 31)

For 1966 I applied for active duty in the Office of Chief of Naval Operations (OP 31) where Dennis Wilkinson (Rear Admiral) was assigned as Officer in Charge of the OP 31 Desk. Dennis was my second skipper on the USS Volador and we were good friends.

When I reported for duty, I found that Dennis had been transferred. Instead of working for Dennis I ended up working for Admiral Pat Hannafin out of the Class of 1944. With my sonar background, Pat asked me to review the work being done on evasion devices for submarines.

The Fleet Ballistic Missile Submarines (SSBN's) were operating out of ROTA Spain and the Russian nuclear submarines were trailing our boats as they entered the Atlantic Ocean. Russian fishing trawlers equipped with sound equipment would make contact on our boats leaving the harbor and vector the Russian submarines to establish contact. Our boats would then spend several days shaking the Russian boats. This made it difficult to maintain schedules of boats on station to fire ballistic missiles.

My assignment was to find out what noise makers, false targets, etc. were available from sonar and ordinance groups in the Navy. I spent a few days talking with various groups in charge of such devices and found that nothing new had been done since World War II.

When I reported this to Pat Hannafin, he asked me to recommend development of tactics and specifications of devices that could be used to help the US Submarine skippers shake the Russian trailers. I wrote a report that suggested the development of low speed devices that would carry a noise generating system that would broadcast the actual recorded noise of the SSBN that was going on patrol. By releasing four or five of these traveling at the same speed as the actual submarine it would give the Russian subs too many targets to track. An additional feature of this device would be to ping back an any signal sent by active sonar.

I concluded that time and money would be wasted if we attempted the noise makers or throwing high speed knuckles that were used in WWII.

Naval War College

My active duty in 1967 was at the Naval War College, Newport , Rhode Island for a two week period of lectures and working with War Game Models. War games are training for senior officers to learn more about strategy and tactics. Red and blue teams work in CIC (Combat Information Centers). We would track opposing forces, control ship and aircraft movements as they would in actual combat.

Of more importance while I was in Newport, the Navy arranged for us to be able to play golf at Newport Country Club after 4:00 PM each day we were there.

Texas A & M

For 1968 the Navy offered two weeks at Texas A &M to learn computer programming for officers. We used a large mainframe computer for 24 hours a day to write cobal and fortran programming. I was planning to put in a computer at Crawford and I wanted to understand the language before we bought a big mainframe.

They also had an 18 hole golf course on the campus. I played every other day.

ComSubLant

In 1969 I again applied to be with my friend, Admiral Eugene P. (Dennis) Wilkinson. Dennis was now Commander Submarine Force Atlantic Fleet.

When I reported to ComSubLant Staff in Norfolk, Virginia, Dennis asked me if I was free to travel during my two weeks active duty. I was willing so he had orders cut for me to go to New London and study the Command Structure there and make recommendations on how the mess could be straightened out. Dennis knew that I had been to Sub School in New London, had duty on the USS Grouper (SS214) and the USS (SSK-1) in New London, had been on active duty with Frank Andrews with ComSubDevGruII in New London and had worked on the Nautilus and Seawolf at Electric Boat in New London.

The various commands in New London were:

1. Commanding Officer of the US Naval Submarine Base

2. Commanding Officer of Submarine School

3. Command of Submarine Development Group II

4. Commanding Officers of Submarine Squadrons Two and Four

5. Commanding Officer of the US Naval Underwater Sound Lab

6. Commanding Officers of Two Submarine Tenders

7. Supervisor of Shipbuilding at Electric Boat Company

8. Commanding Officer of the Submarine Hospital New London (responsible for all research for Submarine Medicine for the whole submarine force)

9. Commanding Officer of the Submarine Repair Base New London

All of these jobs were filled by four stripers (CAPT USN)

of about equal seniority.

I interviewed all of these Captains and wrote a ten page analysis of the conflicts and problems that existed because no one was in charge. I concluded with several possible solutions.

ComSubFlot6, Charleston, South Carolina

In 1971, I learned that Shannon Cramer, Class' 44, had made Admiral and was Commander of Submarine Flotilla Six in Charleston. Shannon and I had been basketball teammates my Plebe Year at the Naval Academy. The prospect of going to Charleston and seeing Shannon appealed to me so I requested assignment there. I received orders for March 1971.

I was thinking I would be assigned some studies about submarine work. But when I arrived at the Flotilla, I found out that Admiral Cramer wanted me to do some studies on Shipyard work at the Charleston Navy Yard.

Besides being an EDO (Engineering Duty Officer) I had extensive experience with both Navy and civilian shipyards. First I was at the Portsmouth Naval Shipyard on Grouper for overhaul in 1947 and then Volador for New Construction in 1948. I was in Mare Island Naval Shipyard to reactivate the Sterlet in 1950. Then I was at Electric Boat Shipyard for K-1 New Construction in 1951, design work on Triton in 1954, Project Officer for Nautilus refueling and Seawolf completion of construction in 1956 and 1957.

I began by interviewing every submarine Commanding Officer in overhaul, all the senior Engineering Duty Officers including the Shipyard Commanding Officer and representative from Naval Reactor, Missile Systems, COMCRUDESLANT (Commander Cruisers, Destroyers Atlantic Fleet) plus others.

The Shipyard Commanding Officer explained to me that the CO's of the submarines were his customers. However when I attended the Shipyard CO's weekly meeting I got a different picture. At these meetings the Submarine CO's would jump to attention and say "Good Morning Sir!". when the Shipyard Commander came in.

I told Shannon Cramer that in civilian business I have never seen a customer jump to attention when the vendor walked into the room.

In Civilian Shipyards, BuShips had a group of EDO's who were commanded by a Captain with the title of Supervisor of Shipbuilding who assisted Submarine CO's in working out problems with the ship's builder. The problem in the Naval Shipyard was that the ship's company on the submarines in overhaul had to do department work during the day and then were being required to witness tests through most of the night, often working 16 or more hours a day. These are the same crews that for years during peace time were gone for 90 day patrols and then in for 90 days. For overhaul time they should work normal days and be able to be with their families.

My report ran 15 pages and was rather complicated. Briefly, I recommended that ComSubLant provide a staff at each Naval Shipyard that could perform the task that the Supervisor of Ship's Building (SupShip) did in Civilian Shipyards.

VICE CHIEF NAVAL OPERATIONS

In April1972 I again applied to work for my friend, Vice Admiral Eugene P. (Dennis) Wilkinson who had now become Vice Chief naval Operations (Submarines). When I showed up at his big office in the Pentagon it was at least 15 paces from the door to the front of his desk. As I was approaching Dennis, he met me half way, shaking my hand. As I sat down he jumped up on his desk, sitting there cross legged like an Indian Chief and exclaimed, "Joe! Tell me what you've been doing."

Dennis set it up so I could go to all the people on his staff and talk over submarine matters. This was of course the area of the Navy that I felt most competent, most able to make a worthwhile contribution and was a fitting finale as my last two-week active duty assignment.

7

1. Make a Product 2. Sell it. 3. Collect & Count the Money

Corporate Challenge

LAYING THE FOUNDATION

I submitted my resignation from the U.S Navy in September 1957, which was the end of my obligated service for the 14 months at MIT in the Nuclear Engineering Program. Rickover approved my resignation subject to a three-month turnover of duties to Rick Claytor, which made my detachment date January 6, 1958.

After submitting my resignation, I sent out resumes to General Electric, Babcock & Wilcox and AVCO, among others. AVCO was involved in the design of the ablative shields for the missile re-entry vehicles. I knew Jack Kyger a Ph.D. who had worked for Rickover and was now Vice President of Research for AVCO. Another possibility was Crawford Fitting Company. The

Chairman and President of Crawford was Fred Lennon, my wife Mary's uncle. I had met him at family affairs over the past ten years. While I was working for Rickover, Fred had come to Washington on several occasions and would take Mary and me out to dinner. He would ask about patent matters and personnel matters at Kenmore Research. Fred also asked me to get in touch with him if I ever decided to resign from the Navy.

My Navy salary was about $12,000 a year when I resigned. AVCO made me an offer of $15,000. Fred offered $6,000. I was preparing to accept the offer from AVCO without even responding to Fred's offer, when Fred called and asked what I was going to do. I told him there was no way I could ask my family to go back to a $6000 a year standard of living. I had decided to accept the AVCO offer and work on the re-entry vehicle's shield design. Fred asked me how much I wanted to work for him. I replied, "At least $14,000." Fred said that would be fine. So I started to work for Crawford Fitting. The major product line was a Swagelok tube fitting which had annual sales of about $2 1/2 million. Two subsidiaries were Nuclear Products Company with sales of only $2,000 and Cajon Pipe Fittings with sales of about $10,000. The parent company name would be changed to Swagelok in 1998.

Fred asked me to go to Kenmore Research in Framingham, Massachusetts as Managing Director. Kenmore was heat treating the steel and stainless steel rear ferrules for the Swagelok fitting and making Blue and Silver Goop. They had been sending the rear ferrules out for copper plating and paying a piece rate for the plating. I put in a plating line which changed Kenmore from a loss operation to a profitable operation.

The main problem that Crawford had at the time was high pull-up torque on stainless steel fittings caused by galling. "Goop" was recommended for preventing the galling but customers did not always use it and therefore had galling on pull-up. What was needed was a lubricant applied to the fitting or the nut that would prevent such galling. I was given the challenge of coming up with a solution.

I tried all kinds of oil based high-pressure lubricants but galling still occurred. It finally dawned on me that a bearing metal was needed. Main shaft bearings on ships were a soft metal so that if the lube system failed, the bearing wiped (smeared) and the main shaft of steel was not damaged. Soft metals act as a very high-pressure lubricant and what we needed for preventing galling was a high-pressure lubricant such as cadmium, tin, silver or gold. Both cadmium and tin worked, but at temperatures around 600 degrees Fahrenheit they caused intergranular corrosion and the base metal disintegrated. Silver had a higher melting point, about 1299 degrees. It was ideal, but it seemed like a high cost way to go. Further study showed that only two ten-thousandths thickness (0.0002) was all that was needed and that only cost about 1/2-cent per nut. So, we became the best stainless steel fitting because proper pull-up could be obtained without galling and a leak tight connection resulted. To hide what we were doing, we wanted the exterior of the nut to still look like stainless steel and just have silver on the threads. We tried rubber plugs and various lacquers or coatings in attempts to strip the silver from the exterior part of the nut while leaving the threads plated with silver. It took two or three months before we were able to strip 20,000 half-inch nuts. Eventually we came up with the process that is still used today to do millions of nuts each year.

It was over ten years before our competitors figured out that we were silver plating the stainless steel nut threads. As a result we became the standard for many large companies because our stainless fittings did not leak. Incidentally, today almost all fitting manufactured use silver plating to lubricate their stainless nuts to prevent galling.

The other program we completed while I was at Kenmore was to design and run test rigs that could run the impulse, vibration, tensile pull and pressure tests of all sizes of fittings in accordance with military specifications that existed at the time for testing fittings. These tests had not been done for our Swagelok fittings and I thought we should run the fittings through these tests just so we could say our fittings passed military specifications.

In October 1958 Fred said I was needed in Cleveland. I responded that I was happy where I was and had plenty of work to do running Kenmore. He offered to double my pay and we moved to Cleveland by the end of October.

When I arrived in Cleveland, Fred took me to Nuclear Products Company. The company was a screw machine company with 12 Brown & Sharpe single spindle screw machines and a turret lathe. Product sales were about $2,000 per year. The machining capacity was used primarily to make parts for Swagelok. Fred showed me their literature on tube plugs and plastic vacuum valves and said, "Congratulations, you are now President of Nuclear Products Company."

I soon found out why Don Steele, my predecessor, had resigned. Fred had sent out instructions to all the distributors of Crawford Fitting to get requests for quotes on anything that their customers wanted machined. Waiting for me on my desk were over fifty of these requests. All required engineering drawings and then costing to be able to quote a price. The problem was that there was no one at Nuclear Products except me to do this work and I figured it would take at least three months just to work up the quotes. And even then the machinery I had could not run the jobs.

We were getting mail addressed to various Nuclear Product Divisions of other companies. So I changed the name of the company to Nupro to avoid the confusion. It was about this time that Fred's son, John Lennon, married Mary Kay Gallagher. Mary Kay's brother, Bernie Gallagher, was a senior at Case Western Reserve University. Bernie started a long association with Nupro by working a few hours after school each day as a draftsman.

Since we already had a sales force selling Swagelok tube fittings I decided that Nupro should be a product company rather than a special order screw machine tool company. I sent all the requests back and notified all distributors to quit asking for quotes. Then I began looking for a product we could manufacture that would be a complement to the tube fittings.

In February 1959 I visited Bill Wilson, our distributor in Los Angeles. While calling on one of his customers I learned from Roger Marsh that the gas chromatography manufacturers in California needed a small metering valve for very low flows. Bernie Gallagher and I worked on the design of something we thought would work. We would make up a sample and send it

Figure 66   Bernie Gallagher and wife, Marty, at North Slope, Alaska.

out. Marsh would tell us why it didn't work and we would try again. After about five prototypes we finally got a design that met all the requirements. In order to get these low metered flows, we used a very long (3/8") small diameter (1/16") orifice and made shutoff on the taper of a 3/8" long, very gradually tapered stem tip. This was not only a patentable design but it is also an almost impossible valve to manufacture. So no one ever tried to copy us. My first patent was granted for a fine metering valve that became an industry standard on all gas chromatographs. By the end of 1960 we were selling 50,000 of these valves a year. Forty years later we are still selling about that many.

In June 1959 Bernie Gallagher and Steve Matousek graduated from Case and joined the company. Bernie was at Nupro and Steve at Cajon. Later in the year, Earl "Squirrel" Shufflebarger and Dave Simko from the same class at Case joined us. At the end of 1959 I was made Executive Vice President of Crawford Fitting Company. In late 1960 Fred asked me to go see what I could do about deliveries at Cajon. I told him the only way I knew of doing that was to move to Cajon and send Earl Wennerstrom from Crawford to run Nupro. Steve and I soon figured out the problems at Cajon. We reduced the number of items on the price list by 50% by eliminating items that had never been sold. We quickly improved delivery.

I was still responsible for Kenmore Research. Noel Hamilton who I had left in charge there was not getting the job done. I asked Steve Matousek to go to Framingham, Massachusetts and take over Kenmore. Steve met his wife, Kathy, in Arlington, Massachusetts. I pulled Earl Wennerstrom from Nupro and put him in charge of Cajon to replace Steve. I then put Bernie Gallagher in charge of Nupro.

In 1961 we decided to bring Kenmore Research to Ohio. We built a facility in Ravenna, Ohio to house the Kenmore work. About

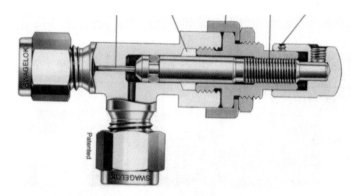

Figure 67   Fine Metering Valve.

that time I decided that Whitey was not performing properly so I moved Steve Matousek to Emeryville, California to take charge of Whitey.

In about 1960 I was making a sales call at AT&T Labs. I would talk about valves or fittings or whatever the people we were calling on wanted to talk about. At that time they had autoclaves making IN23 Crystals that were fed by gas lines. They had various gasses going through the lines and they would change the flows for different effects. AT&T was concerned that if they had an explosion in one autoclave it would go down and blow up the other autoclaves in sort of a chain reaction. What they needed was a valve that would open on very low pressure but would shut off very tight in case they got a high back pressure.

We looked at the problem and designed a half inch check valve specifically for AT&T. Looking around to see who might be another prospect we found that Motorola had a plant in Phoenix that was doing the same type work in autoclaves. We called on Motorola, suggesting they put in the check valves on their gas lines. They declined. About a month later they had an explosion and a bunch of autoclaves went down. We got a rush order for 500 check valves. Bernie and I sat up all night assembling check valves and checking them out so we could take the big order we got from Motorola.

Another check valve application we had was Oak Ridge

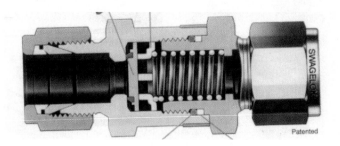

Figure 68   Check Valve.

Tennessee where they were assembling H bombs. We designed a very sensitive valve to relieve a minute amount of gas build up from alpha particles. Testing the valve was very complicated. because of the extremely low pressures. The tests were done in a vacuum with a helium leak test. When Oak Ridge received a shipment from us they would run the tests again. The test were so touchy that there might be three false positives out of a hundred. We had an order for about 1500 which we sent in lots of 100 as they were ready. They would send back the valves that failed their test. After we had shipped about 700 we were told they wanted all the ones they had sent back to us and they would no longer reject any. We decided the reason for this decision was to keep us from knowing the number of Hydrogen bombs that were being produced.

By 1963 Nupro sales were over half a million. If we were going to continue to double every two years, we needed a product with larger potential. We had heard from customers that a positive opening bellows valve was needed. Bellows valves on the market were designed to open by spring force. The spring was compressed when the valve was closed and as the handle was opened, the spring was supposed to open the valve. In many applications, these valves were left closed for quite a time and when you opened the handle the stem stayed stuck in the closed position. Customers told us when the system didn't work right, they would go around and hit all the bellows valves with a hammer to see if they could get the system running again. So we designed a method of positive stem retraction and then helium leak tested all of our bellows valves. Everyone before us had offered helium leak tested valves at an extra charge, maintaining two inventory items.

In four more years our sales were over two million and we were off to the races. By 1995 Nupro was the world leader in bellows valves up to 1" tube size and had sales over $160 million.

While working at Nupro on the product line, I also took over the management of Whitey Company, which Fred bought in 1960. Whitey was manufacturing a small shut-off valve line with sales about $100,000 a year. Valves of this type were tested by a process known as the bubble test. Air pressure of 300 pounds per square inch was applied to the valves while immersed in water. Any leaks would be indicated by air bubbles.

Shortly after I became associated with Whitey an irate customer called and said, "I thought that you 100% bubble tested all of your valves."

I affirmed, "We do."

"Well I just tested some we received from you and they all leak."

I assured him I would look into it. Upon rechecking our test procedures, I determined that a rotating metal stem shut-off to a metal seat galled and would leak after about ten shut-offs. The bubble test was useless. We improved the seat finish and chrome plated the stem of these valves, greatly improving performance. We recommended that such valves only be used on hydraulic oil or other fluids that would provide lubricity at shut-off.

The reason for telling this story was that it led us to a major decision for the future. Steve Matousek and I talked about it and decided in the future all of the new valves we brought out would not have rotation at shut-off. As a result we brought out Cylinder Shut-off valves, Ball valves, Plug valves and the NB valve. The NB valve had a free floating ball in the stem that did not rotate against the seat at shut-off. We never advertised or told anybody that we were doing this, but all new valve designs gave long term, leak tight shut-off. Over the years our decision gave us a product line that always worked and we became the number one company in small valves.

In the Whitey line, I was involved in the design of the NB valve and the Swingaway ball valve. With our decision to make nothing but non rotating seals at shut-off in all future valves, we assigned Ulrich Koch to work on the design. Ulrich was Chief Engineer at Whitey and had worked on valves at the Naval Reactor Branch in Washington. His wife, Opal, was one of Admiral Rickover's secretaries.

On one of my trips to California to check on Whitey, Steve and I were discussing how we might make such a valve. We talked about how great a stellite ball bearing would be for shut-off. It is very hard and has an outstanding finish. On the back of an envelope we sketched drilling out the end of a 4 series valve stem and rolling about a 3/8" by 1/32" cylinder of metal to contain the ball which would rotate in the end of the stem. I said, "Let's try it." We got a stellite ball from the Whitey pump stock of parts. We had Carl Euraneus drill out a stem, roll the metal to retain the ball and test it out. I said, "That's it. Patent it!"

On another trip to Whitey while we were trying to design the 60 series ball valve. Steve and Ulrich asked what I thought about

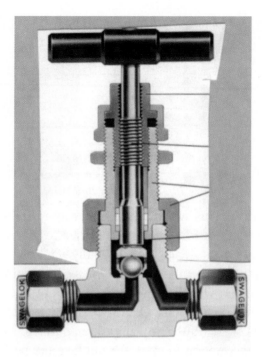

Figure 69   Severe Service Ball Tip NB Shut-Off Valve.

making the 60 series with covered or uncovered bolts. Using uncovered bolts would require less material, save production time and result in lower costs. We were designing this valve for pipe ends up to 1/2 inch and Swagelok ends. I said, "Let's try to connect the uncovered bolt design to a 1/2" pipe by using a pipe wrench on the body." When we tried this we found that one of the uncovered bolts was chewed up by the pipe wrench. I said, "Well we can cover the one bolt and still save the material on the other three." Then we thought, "Hey, if we leave enough clearance, we can remove three bolts and have a swing-away ball valve."

So the Swing Away feature on our ball valve was born. Steve Matousek, Ulrich Koch and myself were the inventors.

Swagelok was the first to use the instructions of "tighten the

Figure 70   Swingaway Ball Valve.

nut 1 1/4 turns". This was an excellent way to tighten a fitting because it used geometry instead of torque to determine proper pull-up. Torque was dependent on many variables, two of the most important being tube wall thickness and tubing hardness. The only problem was that installers would not follow the 1 1/4 turn instructions consistently. Over 95% of all our leakage or blow out problems were caused by improper pull-up. We therefore changed the instruction to mark the nut hex and body hex at the six o'clock position with instructions to pull the nut around to six o'clock and continue to nine o'clock. This reduced the frequency of problems but was not the final answer. After about 20 years in the fitting business, we finally made the fitting gageable so that a gap inspection gage could be used to check the fitting. Getting gageability included tooling and manufacturing changes plus changing the size on all forging so there would be a shoulder to gage to. This took us over five years to put into effect before we could advertise and claim we had gageability. These efforts plus training installers every chance we got made our fitting more dependable than any other in the business.

Moral of the story: We did not just rely on good instructions. We kept trying to find a better way to get field performance and by dogged determination, we ended up getting the best leakage performance in the business.

Figure 71   Ernie Mansour. "Ernie the Attorney".

During the period 1959-60 we had our first attempt to unionize the Company. I had commented on this to several CEO's at Pepper Pike Golf Course that we did not expect the union efforts to be successful. My comment was met with considerable derision. All the companies similar to ours were unionized.

Reese Dill was the labor lawyer who worked with us to be sure we did not have any unfair labor practices. Reese was being assisted by a young lawyer in his firm named Ernie Mansour. Ernie and I became very good friends. We have had hundreds of business meetings and golf games over the years. He is still our corporate attorney today and my closest friend.

I thought of each of our plants operating on the same principle as a 100 crew submarine. That's small enough so the skipper or plant manager knows each crew member personally. Like with submarine officers we had the plant foremen responsible for the training of the workers. We didn't allow a bunch of hollering. If the worker didn't know what to do it was up to the foreman to train him.

My management style is sometimes rather blunt. I don't beat around the bush. I believe in going to the root of the problem, solve it and get on with sales and production. Within the company I am sometimes known as "Sweet Talking Brown" because of the following story.

Willy Jones was driving his pickup truck in the hills of Tennessee and lost control of his truck, hit a tree and was killed. His friends gathered at the local gas station and were bemoaning the death of Willy. One of them said someone must go and break the bad news to Mrs Jones. After some discussion, it was decided that the best person for the job would be Sweet Talking Brown.

So Sweet Talking Brown arrives at the Jones' house and BANG, BANG, BANG, BANG, he raps on the door. Mrs. Jones opens the door. Sweet Talking Brown says, "Are you the Widow Jones?" She replies, "No I am not the Widow Jones." Sweet Talking replies, "The hell you ain't!"

While we were building our new plant for Crawford Fitting Company in 1965 I raised the question about the possibility of air-conditioning the whole plant which would include about 70,000 square feet of manufacturing space. My logic was that in the summer months productivity often went down due to the heat in the plant. Also some of the workers would make statements to management such as "What are you doing out here when you could be in your nice air conditioned office?"

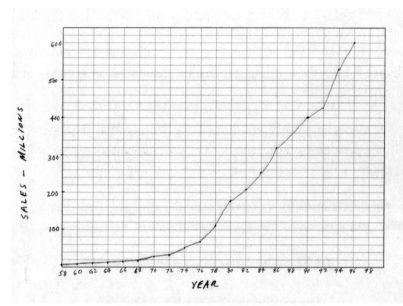

*Figure 72 We have experienced phenomenal growth since 1958. Sales
in millions on vertical axis and the year on the horizontal axis. In 40
years we went from about $2 million to over $600 million.*

When the quotes came in on the cost of air-conditioning the
plant area it looked like a ridiculous thing to do. I asked to see the
specification for the system. I found out that the air- conditioning
was sized for the hottest day of the year for a full 24 hours and
the interior temperature was to remain at 70 degrees. I said get a
quote on the air conditioning capacity to be sized so that the inside
temperature could be maintained 5 degrees below the outside
temperature. This spec cut the tonnage of AC by a factor of 5 and
also the cost by a factor of 5.

In Cleveland, the hottest day is usually 90 and about 75 at
night in actual experience. The spec we used seldom had the plant
above 75 during the hottest day.

We were so pleased with this that we started air-conditioning
all of our plants. It not only improved productivity during the

summer but it also helped stabilize the work force. In Cleveland hardly anyone goes looking for a better job when there is a lot of snow on the ground and we do get a lot of snow. Who wants to change jobs in the summer with a nice clean air-conditioned plant to work in.

It also completely eliminated the feeling that management sat in a nice air-conditioned office while the shop employee had to put up with very uncomfortable heat in the plant.

In 1997 the company was #164 on the Forbes list of 500 top private companies with sales over $600 million. And still union free.

BUILDING THE SALES FORCE

Strong sales cover a multitude of sins.

In November 1958, one month after I became President of Nupro, we had an annual distributors meeting in New York City in the basement of the Essex Hotel. It was in conjunction with the national ISA (Instrument Society of America) show because we sold a lot of fittings to the instrumentation industry. This was my first indication that we needed to start a technical training program for our sales force. From the questions asked it was obvious that the technical competence of the whole organization was fairly low. One question was asked about how much Molybdenum was in 316 stainless steel. Durell Haig who was head of sales at that time replied, "Just a pinch." And when one of our salesmen asked how to respond to customers about questions on the pressure ratings on the fittings, he was told, "Ask the customer what pressure he wanted to operate at. Whatever the customer says you tell him it is fine to handle that." There were no pressure ratings on anything.

One of the early things I did was to start a sales seminar at the factory. About 15 distributors came to the first one. I went over the testing that I had done at Kenmore on tube fittings and talked about pressure ratings and different things along the line of the technical part of fittings. I covered topics such as how to install a fitting, what leakage is and the difference between stainless steel and copper. As the only engineer in the company at that time I got all the trouble shooting work and I was handling all the customer questions. I calculated the various pressure ratings for wall thickness of all the different sized tubing and kept a copy in a drawer of my desk. A lot of time when customers had trouble with something they blamed the fitting. Often the problem would be not the fitting but the fact that some corrosive material had eaten away the fitting. So rather than the fitting itself the problem was the corrosive resistance of the material used to make the fitting. So I had a lot of data on the corrosion resistance of different materials. If I couldn't solve the problem over the phone I would go out in the field and gather information first hand.

From teaching the seminars and dealing with customers' questions I developed the Tube Fitters Manual. We sold thousands of these to our customers. Then when they called up with a question about fittings I would refer them to the page in the manual.

One experience that helped prepare me for teaching the seminars to our sales people occurred during the time I was working for Rickover. For much of that time I was a Lieutenant, not making much money, and it was fairly expensive living in Washington DC. To make ends meet I had a sideline as an adjunct professor at the University of Virginia extension in Washington. I was paid $20 a session teaching one night a week. The classes were held at Washington and Lee High School. Classes were held year round, the three semesters of fall, spring and summer. My courses were generally Algebra, Calculus or Mechanical Technology. Other adjunct professors from Rickover's staff were

Sam Bassett and Sol Levine. Among the three of us if one had to travel or miss a class for some reason one of the other two would cover. I have always been interested in teaching. When I approached management I found out that frequently you solve a lot of problems by approaching them from the standpoint of teaching and training.

Fred Lennon, the owner of the companies, had done a lot of the original selling. The main product was the Swagelok fitting. Fred had a canned speech that he would give while demonstrating the method of putting the tubing in and pulling the fitting up a turn and a quarter. That was fine with the fittings, but now with Nupro and Whitey we were developing a line of valves, which were a little more complicated.

One thing that got us going on training was a distributor in San Francisco named John Van Dyke. John would hire salesmen and then keep them inside for about two months of training before making actual sales calls. We told him that was a waste of time and money. *Obviously*, we thought, the salesman would learn by selling. So the most important thing was to get out in the field making sales calls as fast as possible. But we kept watching Van Dyke and his sales went up faster than anybody else. So we decided we should learn a little bit from him and try to develop better training programs for the sales force.

In 1965 Bernie Gallagher at Nupro was approached by Hugh Beckwith with a suggestion that we try a program learning system for teaching the sales force about valves. Bernie asked me what I thought and I said, "Let's give it a try." Beckwith took the Nupro catalogue and worked up a programmed learning course that was really impressive. He had worked up the course on the products that Nupro had at the time which were bellows valves, check valves, metering valves and a few shut off valves. Within six months of putting out the learning course, Nupro sales were picking up. So we made program learning courses for the Cajon and Whitey lines as well. We also developed programs on cassette tapes keyed to pictures. Later we converted to VCR tapes and now have about 160 tapes for sales training.

Next we needed someone to manage the sales training. As it happened a fellow I knew in the Naval Research Reserve, Dr. Pete Romanoli, became available. Pete had his Ph.D. in Education and was Assistant Superintendent at Orange High School. He got in an argument with the superintendent and asked me if I had anything he could do. Pete came in and set up training schedules for each new salesman that a distributor hired. He was able to mix the stuff up, not spending more than 30 minutes at one time on a given subject, so that 30 days worth of training stayed interesting.

At the same time we were improving the technical knowledge of the salesman, we started trying to make better managers out of the distributors. Our approach to hiring distributors had always been to hire a good peddler. Our emphasis was on sales, not management. Each distributor had an exclusive territory and was required to sell only our products. If they knew the product and knew how to present it, they would get orders. So initially we just wanted the distributors to get us sales orders. But as their business increased they would hire salesmen. And now they were not just peddlers, but also managers.

One of the things I have always said is that I never figured out how to do any of this stuff myself. I just found out who did it right and taught everybody else. We learned from John Van Dyke that if you trained the salesman technically you got more sales. So we had Hugh Beckwith develop the training program and then put Pete Romanoli in charge of training.

The major lesson in sales management came from our distributor in New Orleans, Bob Jennings. Bob was very strong

Figure 73   Bob Jennings, 1980.

on call reports and itineraries. As a result his salesmen sold about twice as much as the other salesmen we had.

Each distributorship is a separate corporation owned by the distributor. They each generated a standard P&L statement that we used in training them to be better managers. Depending on the size of the distributorship we knew the approximate percentage of sales each expense item should be. One of the things we always pushed with the distributors was to pay their salesmen on commission. Our intent was to get the salesman on a 10% commission out of which he would pay his own expenses. Everyone is more careful spending his own money than an expense account. Fred always maintained that a salesman worth his salt would want to be on commission. They always wanted the opportunity to hit the jackpot. Usually at first the salesman would not have enough volume to get by on just commission. So they would start off with a draw plus 5% commission. As soon as they were better off with a straight 10% commission we would recommend that they switch to it.

Another thing we did for the sales force was to sell distributors sample kits for each of the product lines. The samples were cut-aways so the customer could see how the valves and fittings worked. As our product lines grew the kits became so heavy you

Figure 74   With Tom Read, our Houston Distributor.

had to be pretty strong to lug them around. We developed a big catalogue of our products. It cost us about $30 each. We sold them to the distributors for $2 and told them to only give them to their best customers. One distributor, Sam Dibert, bought a thousand of them and put them out to all his customers. Suddenly his sales of Whitey, Nupro and Cajon jumped up in comparison to everyone else. This was in the period we were expanding from just Swagelok fittings to valves. The salesmen were not pushing the valves. But when the customer had the catalogue they would buy the valves anyway. When we saw what happened with Dibert, we changed our tune and told all the distributors to get a catalogue

Figure 75   Bill Roach, "The Coach".

out to all their customers. That was a big help in expanding our product lines.

About 1964 Bill Roach came with the company. Fred hired Bill because he was the golf pro at Sea Island. Fred's idea was that Bill would play golf with our customers and get more business that way. But Bill wanted to show that he could be effective working with the distributors. He became the key person in hiring new distributors and training the distributors. He convinced me that I should go with him because the distributors would pay more attention with me along. So he and I started flying around the country meeting with distributors. We would meet with three a day, fifteen a week. In this way I met all the distributors every two years, half one year and half the next. Later Bill and I visited the European distributors each year and followed the same agenda we used in the U.S.

We called ourselves the "Huntley-Brinkley" team. That was a 15-minute nightly news broadcast on NBC popular at the time. Bill and I would double up on the distributor. First Bill would make a pitch about the things that were working well for other distributors and when he got tired I would start talking. Seeing three distributors a day, we had the most time with the last distributor because we would be staying over. We would usually take the distributor and his wife out to dinner at a nice place. We always arranged that the last distributor of the day would either be one with high production or low production. We liked to have extra time to learn the secrets of the ones with high production so we could pass it on. And on the ones with low production we used the time to emphasize how profitable the other distributors were getting by using the call reports, itineraries, sample kits, catalogue and sales training.

We really evolved a super sales training program. It was so good in fact that we ended up training most of our competitors. But that was all right. The ones that left were not the best ones, so we didn't mind that they left.

Bill Roach was a very important man in helping build our distribution system. He retired on January 1, 1985 and died on January 8, 1991. We called Bill "the Coach" because he taught us some golf and also coached the distributors.

In 1961 I made a trip to Europe. Going through Germany, France and the United Kingdom I got some idea of the amount of industry there that would be good prospects for our products. On returning I mentioned to Fred that we should consider at least getting a toehold in Europe.

The following year we had a trade show in Pittsburgh. A couple of Europeans came to our booth and decided they wanted to represent us. One was Jacques Bargain from Paris and the other was Bronco Weiss from Zurich. Jacques had a company named Techmation and Bronco had Kontron. Each company had about 28 engineer type salesmen plus mechanics. They provided a warranty service for analytical instruments and were already using our parts. I think they figured if they were distributors for us they would be getting distributor prices and would make more money on repairs.

The problem for us was that Bronco and Jacques both covered some of the same territory. So we divided it up so Jacques had Belgium, the Netherlands, France and the UK. Bronco had Germany, Switzerland and Austria.

After we got to doing a fair amount of business with both Techmation and Kontron we took a closer look and decided we were not getting nearly as much business as we could. Lawrence Shavick, the Techmation man who ran the London office only had 8 salesmen. Lawrence maintained that was all he needed for all of the United Kingdom. We strongly disagreed. I made a few sales calls with Dave Cheetham, one of the salesmen in the London office. Dave felt like we were missing all kinds of opportunities and he would like to help us get better established. Rather than get in an argument with Techmation I suggested that Dave go up to Scotland and start a distributorship.

Dave agreed although his real objective was to go back to his hometown of Manchester. We agreed that if he did a good job in Scotland we would see about getting him to Manchester. As the off shore oil drilling swung into high gear Dave opened offices in Glasgow, Aberdeen and Edinburgh. The next place we opened up was Teeside and Dave helped us find Johnny Walker to go there. Then we moved Dave down to Manchester and we also opened

Figure 76   Dave Cheetham with his wife, Pat.

Bristol with John Dare. We divided London into a north and south district and gave Alan Tinker the south side. Lawrence Shavik kept north London for another ten years with his eight salesmen at a time when we had over 50 salesmen in the UK. We eventually put Mike Brereton in the North London district. We found Luc

Figure 77   Wolf Ast.

Wouters for Belgium and Franz Perquin for the Netherlands leaving Jacques with just France.

Basically the same evolution took place with Bronco. We changed the Austrian territory to an independent distributor. Then Hoffman la Roche bought Kontron and became our distributor in Germany. Kontron had put salesmen in all the major cities in Germany with a main office in Munich operated by Wolf Ast. Wolf came to me and said he didn't think Hoffman la Roche, a very large chemical-drug company headquartered in Switzerland, really wanted to be bothered with selling our tube fittings. He would be interested in becoming a distributor. He negotiated with Hoffman la Roche and bought the distributorship. Wolf had hired the salesmen so most of them came with him. Several years later, in each large city, the salesman was offered a distributorship. So we ended up with six distributorships in Germany. Wolf retained the distributorship in Munich.

Figure 78   Chen Tong Chua with wife, Siew Eng Chua.

We hired Jose Ingatio Gonzalez Lopez in Madrid to handle Spain and Fiorenza Manza in Florence to supply Italy. About this time we also opened up Australia. At a trade show we were approached by a fellow by the name of Koshiba who wanted to help us develop Japan. Koshiba opened an office in Osaka. We now have eight distributors and about 100 salesmen in Japan. Having reached all the way out to Japan, Singapore began to look inviting. We were approached by a Chinese fellow named Chen Tong Chua who wanted to open a distributorship in Singapore.

Figure 79   Wolf Ast and his wife, Rosemarie.

After only nine months, Chen wanted to open eight more distributorships. Bernie Gallagher and I went over to talk to him and find out just what he needed. We liked him so we asked him to open offices in Indonesia, the Philippines, Hong Kong, Kuala Lumpur and Bangkok.

In 1988 I made a trip around the world and held a special awards ceremony in four cities to honor these men who helped me cover the world. Special honorary certificates went to Koshiba in Osaka, Chen Tong Chua in Singapore, Wolf Ast in Munich and Dave Cheetham in Manchester.

The places that we elected not to go into were generally places

Figure 80   With Kazuo Koshiba in Tokyo, November 1980.

Figure 81   Kimie and Kazuo Koshiba.

that had laws saying if someone in the country was making a fitting or valve you were not allowed to import. Someone might be making just a few valves in a garage, but that was enough to preclude imports. This was the case in India and much of Latin America. Generally in these countries there was an exception in that the governments could buy imports. We decided not to deal in countries where the officials were corrupt and bribes were customary. Also we avoided the Middle East because of all the fighting. In some cases I let our distributor in New York, Bob Crum, hire agents to supply places that we did not want to establish a distributorship.

As sales continued to build I needed to turn my attention more and more to production which was falling behind.

BUILDING PRODUCTION

An efficient work force with a high state of morale is essential to the success of any enterprise.

One of the things we started early on was to have shop talks with the employees. At first they were almost every Friday. Later we cut back to twice a month and now it is generally once a month. We have a coffee break each day from 9:00 to 9:15. On the mornings that we had shop talks we would just extend the coffee break an additional 15 minutes so the shop talk would be from 9:00 to 9:30.

In these shop talks we communicated to the employees safety problems, production problems, how fringe benefits programs worked, any new plans we were considering, etc. We also tried to give the employees the big picture so they would feel a part of the company. For example we talked about all the different product lines and who our major customers were. And of course the employees could ask questions and make suggestions for topics to be covered in future shop talks. So this gave us a good basis for being able to discuss problems we were having and to get the employees to where they felt they were part of the business.

After we started with our sales training, sales increased fairly rapidly and we started to have delivery problems. We decided we should look at production training because if training helped so much with sales maybe we could improve our production considerably. The only method in place was a sort of buddy system. An employee who had been working a few years would take a new employee under his wing and teach him how to run a machine. A major problem with this was that any existing bad practices would be continued on by the buddy system.

In preparation for a training program I called a meeting of all the foremen to find out what they considered to be the main problems in training new employees. There was continual feed back that we were hiring lousy new employees who could never learn how to operate a machine. The foremen complained that new employees frequently did not know fractions, decimals and angles that they should have learned in high school. After talking to the foremen I concluded that it was unrealistic to expect the foremen to be teachers. They tended to assume too many things that the new employee should know. They would use shop terminology such as reamer, collet and chuck and because they had been using the terms for 20 years couldn't believe that some did not know what they meant. The new employees didn't ask what the words meant for fear of appearing dumb. As a result the foreman would conclude the employee was not hired properly and couldn't learn how to operate the machine.

Knowing what we had learned in sales training, we started with programmed learning courses in fractions. We confined fractions to 1/64, 1/32, 1/16 and up because that is all we had on our manufacturing drawings. We taught only adding and subtracting these fractions because that is all that was needed. Then we taught decimals, degrees and angles and how to use micrometers. Shop terms were a foreign language to most new employees. So we made a programmed learning course of shop terms to give new employees a shop vocabulary so they could understand the instructions they would receive on the shop floor. These courses were given during the first 30 days after a person

Figure 82   Ed Holt did an outstanding job setting up plant training programs.

was hired and they would be tested before they went on a machine.

For several years I had been getting calls from Ed Holt, a

submariner and Naval Academy classmate. Ed was frustrated with his job at Electric Boat and would call wanting to know if I had anything he could do. I knew that if I hired him I would have to give him something significant that he could make a real contribution. In the Navy we were always helping the sailors study to strike for their next rate. So I knew Ed would understand what we were putting in place. Fortunately he called again just as we were starting the training program and I said, "Ed, I've got just the job for you."

In our shop talks we explained to everyone that we were going to go to a more intense training program. We explained that one of the purposes was to be fair with everyone. One of my firm beliefs and a saying I have been noted for over the past 30 or so years is "You can't require performance unless a person knows how to do the job. He also has to know what is expected of him." Under the old system we were teaching without the teacher really being qualified to teach. After a few years the foreman would say the employee knew what he was doing even if he didn't, because otherwise it would be a bad reflection on the foreman. When the employee was not confident of his job knowledge he would have anxiety about the possibility of being fired for not knowing. So fairness to the employees was a big part of the training program.

First I felt we could not risk demoralizing the foremen by implying they didn't know what they were doing. It was a rare foreman who knew how to teach. Instead of writing a procedures manual we developed a video that demonstrated proper machining procedures. As we developed the videos we showed them first to the foremen to get their comments. That way all the foremen were brought up to speed on proper procedures as we were preparing the training program.

We also taught foremen how to be teachers. We started a program where each employee had his own spread sheet that documented the extent of his skill with the different machines and gave skill points for each task. The spread sheet would begin with *"Know how to turn machine on"* which would be worth perhaps one point. *"Setting a drill"* might be worth several points and *"Setting a threading attachment"* might be worth six points. Across from each task was a place for the employee to sign and for the foreman to date and sign.

We had another chart that used total skill points to determine hourly pay. Skill points were plotted on the horizontal axis and hourly rates on the vertical axis. We emphasized at the shop talks that we wanted to be fair with everybody. The ones who knew the most could produce the most and would make more money than the people who could not do that. As long as we had a logical fair system people were willing to go along and work as hard as they could to become more productive employees. We very seldom had people quit and leave the company after they had been with us two years. By that time we had taught them to be a highly competent machinist. They understood how the system worked and appreciated the amount of effort we put into making the system fair and getting everyone to making the highest wage they were capable of. This all contributed to high corporate morale and high productivity.

The next step in our efforts to increase productivity involved Lenny Spontelli, a true engineering genius. Lenny and Ed Holt worked on the CAPE program, which stands for Computer Assisted Production Engineering. Spontelli went through and calculated all the factors involved in machining. By looking at all the variables he could determine how hard you could work the machine before it would begin to fail, either from the temperature of the drill or some other factor.

One of the things we wanted to do was eliminate repeat problems and to get everybody to avoid some of the problems we had run into as we ratcheted up production. We decided that one of the things was a lot of our machinery was fairly old. If a man had a machine that wasn't performing properly he could not keep up with the work of somebody that had a machine in better condition. So we went through what we called qualifying a machine, measuring its performance to know what could be expected from it and determining its optimum operating process. By qualifying a machine we got rid of loose bearings and improper machine performance. The machine became less of a problem in causing rejects. Ten or more years after we did this, a highly touted system called SPC (Statistical Process Control) became well known. It had a first step which was "qualifying the machine".

We came up with fast methods of setting tools so it would take less time to change a tool. We improved our gauging methods so that we could gauge faster and again make the machine run better. We knew that the tools were not as consistent as we desired. So I sent Len Spontelli and Bill Cosgrove to Toner, our tool shop for manufacturing our tools, with the mission of automating as much as possible the manufacture of the tools. With automation we would increase the consistent quality of the tools. In this way we took the average life of a seating reamer from seven hundred pieces up to around ten or fifteen thousand. We significantly increased production by controlling our own manufacturing of the tools.

We also looked for ways to automate production. One success was in creating an automatic loader for our chuckers. All the chuckers operated by having an operator take a forging and putting it in the chuck by hand. This was not only slow but dangerous. It didn't happen often, but this is where you lose a finger. It was possible for the operator to close the chucker while still holding the forging. Also in loading the chuckers the operators were subject to come in contact with the cutting oil which would cause dermatology problems. Developing the automatic loading avoided these problems.

***Figure 83   Bill Cosgrove, now President of Swagelok, is counting
his winnings from me on the golf course.***

I put Bill Cosgrove in charge of improving the productivity of our machines. I always gave Bill the toughest jobs because he always seemed to get it done. Consequently he is now running the company.

Our production rates on a lot of these items were not just minor increases. Some cycle times were changed from 24 seconds to 9 seconds, an improvement of 267%. We controlled costs considerably by training the people to be able to work at these higher speeds improving the tools and improving the performance of our machines. Our increased productivity was evidenced by the fact that we did not increase prices from 1985 to 1992 even though we had increasing costs of material and labor.

Another factor affecting our improved production was our success at vertical integration. In our business if you don't have the parts for two or three months you are liable to lose the business for 15 years. So you cannot afford to not have the routine items available all the time. We had been having our brass parts made by Mueller Brass. We got a lot of rejects from them. And we were constantly sending people up to show them the quality we wanted and inspect their work. All of a sudden in 1972 Mueller said, "We are not going to make your stuff anymore. We are not going to finish the orders we have. Good Bye."

Fortunately we were already machining 316 stainless steel. The 316 is more difficult to machine than the 300, the 303 and the 304 that other people were machining. 316 stainless wears the tools out faster and it is tough to get a good finish. By comparison, brass is easy to run.

To handle the emergency of the loss of supplies from Mueller Brass we were able to convert some machines from running 316 to running brass. Eventually we took one plant and gradually built it up to where it ran all our brass parts for the tube fittings.

Another problem occurred with our supplier of forged parts for elbows, tees and crosses. In forging you have a flashing where the trim is cut off and we always wanted the forging made to very tight tolerances so that the chuck could hold it properly. Otherwise you might damage the chuck in manufacturing. So we were constantly trying to get our supplier to improve the quality. The final straw was when we had bought stainless steel for the forger to use during the time of a threatened steel strike. When the steel strike happened he started using our stainless steel for other customers thinking he could replace it before he needed to supply us. However he was not able to replace it in time and left us short.

I decided no one was ever going to do that to us again. We bought forging machines and started learning how to make our own forgings. As a result we were able to keep them to a tighter tolerance which helped our production.

As demand for our products grew because of quality production and a highly trained sales force we built over 30 manufacturing plants including one each in Switzerland, Canada and the United Kingdom. We manufacture over 6,000 standard items which we maintain in five warehouses, two in the US and one each in Lachen Switzerland, Osaka Japan and Sydney Australia.

As we grew I knew that we would need to be computerized to maintain the quality organization we were creating. We went into computers in 1965 before software was available. At first we had to write our own programs and make inputs with punched cards. We are now on our third generation of computers. We are able to bring up on a screen any of our thousands of parts and see how many were bought in the past year from each of our five warehouses and the current inventory at each warehouse.

Originally our business was paper intensive with eight copy snap out forms and all orders coming in by mail. In 1966 we required all of the distributors to start sending their orders in by Novar. Novar used compressed transmission to send orders over telephone lines in a fraction of a minute. This cut four days off our delivery time.

In 1968 we set an objective to use computers to become completely paperless in handling all of our orders. Today we receive all of our orders into our computer from the distributors' computers. We do not print the order. To pull parts for shipment we have a 24 foot high, automatic warehouse retrieval system that delivers the parts to a packer. The packer scans the bar code against the order on the PC screen. The shipping label is generated and automatically slapped on the box as it moves down the conveyor line to the correct position for pickup and shipping. We do not print a shipping copy or an invoice. These are sent electronically to the distributor's computer. If he wants copies he can print them.

My final objective in computerizing our sales and accounts receivable process was achieved in January 1996. Fifteen days after shipment we had the payment electronically transferred from the distributor's bank account to the company bank account. In the whole process the only paper printed was the address label. It was a complete digital process from receiving the order to collecting the money. Largely because of the automated process we are shipping at 99.8% accuracy.

In 1994 we began scanning incoming paper that needed to be stored. That first year we stored on CD's the information on 1,300,000 pieces of paper which saved us the expense of 360 file cabinets. In six years we figure we will get rid of 2000 file cabinets and have much quicker retrieval of needed information from electronic filing.

We have come a long way since I joined the company in January 1958. At that time we were producing one product, a patented tube fitting with annual sales of less than $3 million. Today, preparing to enter the 21st century, we have over 6,000 products and sales over $600 million. In the next chapter I will talk about our corporate philosophy that made this possible.

8

People are known by the company they keep. A company is known by the people it keeps.

Corporate Philosophy

The reason for the success of the Swagelok Companies was in large part due to the corporate philosophy that we were able to inculcate in all areas of activity. When we started our employee training programs, I was asked to give a talk on our Company Philosophy. I tried to think of all the things that we did to run a great operation. Finally the light came on and I realized that our objective was to do everything first class. We emphasized at every opportunity that we were a first class company, of first class ladies and gentlemen, making first class products. We started by having each new employee see a video in which I gave the following speech.

Welcome to Swagelok. We believe that you are now a member of the best manufacturing and sales organization. You produce or sell the best products and you work with the best group of people you have ever met. This "being best" hasn't just happened by accident. We have a company objective of doing all of our business first class. It is our intention in designing and manufacturing our products to make them better than any competitors' products. Our products are designed to do the job; they are not designed to beat a price. We manufacture to close tolerances and use rigid quality control procedures so that the performance designed into our products is there in every item we sell. Sometimes people speak of our fittings or valves as being too good for their applications or refer to Swagelok as the Cadillac of the tube fitting industry. Our competitors will often attempt to sell by telling the customer that he doesn't need anything as good as Swagelok.

We are thus in a very enviable position and it is one that we have worked hard to achieve. The recognition by our customers and our competitors that we are the best. When you are in our plants you can see what we mean by a first class operation. They are modern, extremely well lighted, air conditioned and maintained at a cleanliness level that is unheard of in machine shops. Our visitors have often said that our plants are so clean you could eat off the floor. Such first class conditions enable us to attract the best people to manufacture our products and insure low turnover of personnel. In our precision machinery we use the highest quality tooling, materials and cutting oil that can be purchased. This combination of superior plant conditions and facilities creates an atmosphere where in everyone knows he is expected to work to close tolerances and produce the highest quality products. As a first class organization it is our policy to be completely fair with everyone, our customers, our distributors our salesmen and our office and plant employees. To operate fairly with the customer we must furnish him with valves and fittings, which perform reliably at a price he can afford to pay. The fact that we have sold more valves and fittings every year that we have been in business would indicate that the customer knows he is getting his money's worth.

Our distributors don't have to worry about our having house accounts, because we don't sell direct to any customers. All of our sales are handled through our independent distributors. The distributor has an adequate margin for him to hire good office personnel, maintain a proper inventory, pay his salesmen, cover business expenses and retain enough profit so the distributorship will continue to grow. The salesman who works for the distributor must be able to make a good living so he will continue selling our products. Our sales are made by personal calls. And without successful salesmen in the field neither the distributor nor the factories can be successful.

Just as fundamental to our overall success is a well trained, satisfied plant or office employee, earning sufficient income so that he or she is proud to continue manufacturing our products. We believe that a first class organization recognizes and meets these needs for fairness to all. The usual way others do business is to let expediency dictate the organization's policies. If the customer insists on a lower price, the order would be handled direct from the factory and the distributor by-passed, or the salesmen's commission would be reduced, or the plant and office employees would be under paid, or inventories would be maintained at an inadequate level to effectively service the customer. We believe it is poor business and unfair to do these things. We will stick to our policy of fairness and not be governed by expediency.

Lets look further into some other factors that contribute to our first class image. Our overall planning must include research, design, introduction of new products, and expansion of facilities while providing for reasonable profit. Our overall sales effort includes product samples, magazine advertising, catalogs and displays at many national shows. Our product samples are not polished or made especially as samples. They are the way we make all of our products, better than anyone else. Our advertising is in

213

good taste and factual. It is advertising of which we can all be proud. Our catalogs and data sheets are the best that can be produced, they are much better than any competitor has available. All of these things help to build our image of always being first class.

But most important it is first class people that make a first class organization. You will find that our group of salesmen and distributors are clean-cut, hard-hitting salesmen whom you will enjoy meeting, and they are people you certainly wouldn't want to sell against. Our factory personnel, both plant and office are truly dedicated to quality performance. Our people really enjoy what they are doing, they are truly proud of their work and they keep our organization on top.

To summarize, our organizations prime objective is a constant dedication to always being first class. First class people, first class product design, first class product quality, first class methods of doing business, first class sales tools which include product samples, advertising and catalogs, first class inventory control and stocks to service our customers, and most important, a first class attitude among all our people insuring a first class future for us all. Welcome aboard. You are here because you are first class!

This program was shown to all new factory employees and all new distributor employees as part of their indoctrination. I thought this would get people started off with the right attitude about the type of company we are.

In our training programs for foreman and plant managers, I tried to pass on a lot of my beliefs about how to treat people. My starting point is… ***"You require performance in a nice way!"***

Don't try to hire perfect people. You will not find them. We hire the best we can get and then train them well, both in job

Figure 84   Our Swagelok headquarters in 1965.

skills and our corporate culture. We do not have janitors in the factories. Our employees are responsible for cleaning their own work areas and common areas are cleaned by teams of employees. In this way we have gained a reputation for having immaculate work areas. Once a visitor was walking through the plant and dropped a cigarette butt on the floor. A nearby machine operator tapped him on the shoulder and said, "Sir, we don't do that here."

In one of our plants we use about 200 machines made by Warner & Swasey. Sometimes when the machines are not running as well as we think they should we call Warner & Swasey and have them send an engineer over. On one occasion the engineer was working on the machine and commented to our machine operator, "The problem with you people is you are just too picky. We don't get this many calls from other companies."

Our machine operator replied, "When you are the best, you learn to be picky."

In 1989 when I started to turn the operation of the Company over to Steve Matousek, I decided we should commence strategic

The Swagelok companies Mission Statement

Our mission is to be the best supplier, worldwide, of the highest quality fluid system components readily available to industry and supported by service that is technically sound, customer driven, and of the highest integrity.

In accomplishing this mission, we will...

...remain union free by maintaining a culture that values and recognizes the individual and one that is based upon fairness in all of our employee relationships.

...promote an "esprit de corps" by including all employees as part of a team which enjoys competition and has fun in the process.

...hire the best people we can find and develop their abilities to the highest level possible.

...sell and service through a sales organization that exclusively stocks and distributes our products.

...continually improve our methods to lower costs and remain competitive, utilizing the best technology. Our philosophy is that everything can be done better.

...achieve quality in all aspects of our business operations.

...provide new products to meet the needs of our customers and new technologies.

Figure 85   Our Mission Statement continues to serve us well.

planning and started by writing our Mission Statement. It is on the preceding page.

I will close this chapter with a brief excerpt from a speech I gave at Hillsdale College in March 1998 which pertains to our corporate philosophy.

"......If you are in business you are in the people business. When I left the Navy, I came out convinced that if the Marine Corps could have an esprit de corps when they were asking people to jump out of a foxhole to be shot at, I could have and esprit de corps in a company when I was only asking people to manufacture tube fittings and valves in a nice clean air conditioned plant.

"......As an ex-submariner, I knew that with submarine crews of about 100 it was possible for the Captain to know every crew member by his first name and also know the names of their children. Morale aboard a submarine was very high compared to a battleship largely because no one was just a number. Therefore our plants were sized to employ about one hundred and we hired plant managers to be our submarine captains. The captains like to run their own show and are measured for performance and the employee is not lost in a crowd. We have over 3000 production employees who have never missed one hour's pay for lack of work. We are a union free company. And we are very proud of these records.

"........To achieve esprit de corps amongst workers you must follow some common sense approaches My first rule is you never expect a person to perform a job unless he knows how to do the job. This seems pretty simple. But you find managers and foremen around the world hollering at people who have not been trained, don't know how to do their job and don't know what is expected of them. At Swagelok our supervisors are trained never to raise their voice in anger with our employees You cannot scare someone into

217

doing a good job. We expect all of our employees to be polite at all times we always refer to our employees as ladies and gentlemen and that is the sign you see on all of our restroom doors.

"Each employee has his (or her) name at his work station in the same design holder that I have on my desk. Each employee also has his first name on his shirt. This makes everyone feel recognized and it also makes it possible for me to call people by their first name when I am in the plant.

"To maintain esprit de corps you must communicate. For over thirty years we have had shop talks in everyone of our plants during Friday morning coffee breaks. Normally coffee break is fifteen minutes but for Friday morning shop talks we make it thirty minutes. We cover such subjects as fringe benefits, plant safety, production, quality, competition, sales and any topic our employees ask to be discussed.

"Our objective is to make our employees members of our team. All Americans like to compete and be on the winning team. We explain why our products are better, where our products are used and how we are doing. By communicating our workers become part of our winning team. To be a winner you must have someone to beat. And of course that is our competition. Some people need someone to hate. I have always felt I would prefer to have my employees hating the competition rather than our managers and supervisors.

9

It is better to make decisions, even if wrong, than to spend all your time trying to avoid mistakes.

Entrepreneurship

The first investment I made in new companies or startups was the formation of Midwest Bank & Trust in 1967. I knew Ray Rossman, a Cleveland banker who had been with Central National. Ray asked me if I wanted to be an investor in a new bank he was putting together. His plan was to raise two million from investors putting in a minimum of $100,000 each. At our company we dealt with many small businesses Their banking experience indicated to me there could be a market for a new bank. Many of our suppliers would have companies with one to two million in annual sales. The owner would be making about $100,000 in annual salary plus a company profit of $100,000 to $200,000. These were good solid businesses. But when they went to the bank for loans they were considered high risk and treated like nobodies. We envisioned Midwest Bank & Trust going after the middle to small size companies run by people we knew. Also we had the involvement of Monsignor Edward Seward, Financial Secretary of the Cleveland Catholic Diocese and priest of St.

Clement Catholic Church in Lakewood. The bank would handle a lot of the Bishop's funds which was a good base.

So I scraped together everything that I didn't need and put $250,000 into Midwest Bank. I split up the investment with each of the three kids and Mary, so we were actually five stockholders. I was asked to go on the Board of Directors and the bank was very successful. About ten years later we sold the bank to Provident of Cincinnati. The original $250,000 was worth about $900,000. On the sale we took a 20 year note at 17% interest. It was during the period of Carter's presidency with high inflation and interest rates. We stipulated in the note that the full 17% interest would have to be paid even if the note were paid off early. Of course after President Reagan took office interest rates and inflation came down and that turned out to be a good deal.

Having been involved in the bank I became interested in other businesses of the type that looked like they had a future. But the next venture did not turn out so good. Two friends, A. O. Rule and Noel Davis asked me to be on the Board of Directors of their company, Environmental Growth Control. Rule is a Naval Academy graduate and Davis is a graduate of MIT. Since I had graduated from both they put me on the board to settle disputes between them. The company manufactured growth control chambers, which would control the lighting, temperature and humidity. They were used by research facilities working on growing seedlings for the paper industry and other plant growth research. They investigated how you could fool plants into growing faster by having shorter days. With six hours of day light followed by six hours of dark, the plant was tricked into having two days of growth in one 24 hour period.

Noel Davis developed the idea of a hydroponics plant factory as a new business. It seemed like a great idea. The company was called Phytofarms of America. The plant factory was housed in a

Figure 86   L-R: A. O. Rule and my brother, John Callahan.

large structure that covered an acre and raised leaf lettuce, spinach and various herbs. Noel developed a helix drive that would take the trays from one end of the building to the other, increasing the width between the trays as the plants grew. I had put about a million dollars in the business when we finally closed it down in 1975.

One night in 1979 Bill Jones called. Bill was a neighbor in Daisy Hill where I live. I had met him at various parties. The deal Bill presented called for a $100,000 investment from me to join in the purchase of Invacare, a wheel chair manufacturing company owned by Technicare, a subsidiary of Johnson and

Johnson. At that time Invacare had annual sales of about $19 million. Bill told me that Everest & Jennings (E&J) was the leader in the field and had about 80% market share. Invacare was the second largest with 10% market share and the other 10% was a group of 15 to 20 small players. I told Bill that I liked the chance of moving number two into having a larger market share.

Technicare made diagnostic imaging products for hospitals, including Computer Tomography, (CAT), Nuclear and MRI Scanners. Wheelchairs didn't really fit into their high tech image. And Johnson & Johnson was not paying much attention to it. After we made the purchase, Mal Mixon, who had been VP Marketing at Technicare, was named President and I was on the Board of Directors. Other original investors besides Bill Jones, Mal and myself were Dan Moore, Whitney Evans and J. B Richey. They were all friends of Mal's and became active Directors of the company. Stan Pace, President of TRW, was recruited by Bill Jones and Larry Robinson, head of a jewelry store chain, was recruited by Mal Mixon as additional investors.

Mal asked for my help in manufacturing and I became his right hand man in that area. I told Mal that he couldn't do everything himself and that he had to find six to eight real strong managers to help him run the company. Over the years, he has put together a strong senior management group which today consists of Jerry Blouch, Tom Miklich, Lou Slangen, Larry Steward and "JB" Richey. JB is a genius engineer and Mal was able to talk him into leaving Technicare and become head of Engineering and Research at Invacare. JB's leadership has resulted in technical leadership in the Home Healthcare field. His patents have helped move Invacare to the top company in the business.

At one point Mal needed legal help in dealing with a contract with the VA. I suggested my attorney, Ernest P. Mansour. Ernie became Invacare's corporate attorney and now spends about half

*Figure 87   With, L-R, Ernie Mansour, Mal Mixon and Bill Weber
July 1993, my 70th birthday party.*

his time on Invacare business. Another time Mal wanted me to get involved in buying a building. I said, "Mal, I don't know anything about buying buildings, I've never gotten involved in that. But I know a guy you should talk to. Bill Weber is a good man in industrial real estate." From there Bill became a member of the Board of Directors of Invacare. Mal also ended up with another friend of mine, Jim Boland CPA with Ernst and Young, to do our accounting work. So Invacare used these advisors I had. One thing you have to learn in business is to have good advisors. Mansour, Weber and Boland have all been a big help to the company for many years.

Mal had Pat Nalley to run the sales force. Pat was a retired executive from Harris Corporation where Mal had worked for Pat as a salesman, sales manager and Director of Marketing. With Mal's natural skill in marketing our sales grew rapidly.

In the "I'd Rather be Lucky than Good Department" one of the things that helped us grow so fast was a problem that developed at E&J, our main competitor. We were all optimistic about Invacare because the demographics of the aging population would insure growth in the industry. E&J had the same information and were building a large new plant as they closed their old plants. We got started about the time E&J was moving into their new plant. Their deliveries suffered because they were not up to speed in the new plant. We were able to move into the gap and take over the growth. E&J started losing money because they did not get the growth they planned for their new plant.

As a result of our excellent marketing, outstanding product development and great leadership by Mal Mixon, our sales rose to over $300 million. We decided to take Invacare public in 1984. My $100,000 investment paid off quite well. In fact at today's share price of $24, the $100,000 investment is worth over $40 million.

In 1980 I got a call from Bud Talbot, another friend who lives on Shaker Boulevard just down the road from Daisy Hill where I live. Bud wanted to know if I would be interested in helping him and a group buy Sawyer Research. Sawyer had sales of $2 million a year in quartz crystals used in CB radios and watches. The company had 200 autoclaves where they grew the quartz crystals. The process is to take a seed crystal, put it in the autoclave with raw quartz, take the temperature up to 550 degrees, the pressure up to 4000 pounds and let crystals grow on the seed. The process is very similar to the high school experiment of growing sugar crystals on a string, only on a much larger scale..

I invested $100,000 and went on the Board of Directors. During the period we owned the company, annual sales increased to about $12 million. We were doing well and demand for the crystals was outgrowing our ability to supply. I wanted to expand the volume but other members of the board didn't want to make the investment. So I said we either expand or sell out. They decided we would sell to somebody in Taiwan. So I tripled my investment after a couple of years, which was OK but nothing like Invacare.

John Balch was an accountant who had worked with Mal Mixon at Technicare. In 1981 John came to Mal Mixon with a possible deal. Royal Appliance was a company founded in the 1800's. They made vacuum cleaners and had competed for years with Hoover. Royal failed to shift to plastic from all metal vacuum cleaners after WWII and their sales fell to about $6 million annually. Mal and I got three investors each and bought the company. John became President. My investment was $60,000 for 1/8 of the company.

Besides large upright vacuum cleaners they were making a hand held vacuum cleaner out of metal. In looking over there sales records, we noted that they were running out of these hand held vacuums at Christmas every year. We decided to make them out of plastic which was much cheaper and make enough so we wouldn't run out. The first model we came up with was a red plastic hand vacuum with a red bag. Someone suggested we call it the Dirt Devil. I said, "Trademark that name, that sounds good to me." Black and Decker had a hand held battery powered vac that they called Dust Buster and it was a very popular item. We thought that our 110-volt motor with a rotating brush would do a much better job.

The most hand vacs the company had made in the past was 20,000 units for the Christmas season, October through December. We decided to make 100,000 thinking that would be plenty. It wasn't enough so the next year we made 300,000. And we ran out again. Then we got Wal-Mart and K-Mart interested and we started making 5 million a year. We added uprights and other models all in red plastic, but the real base of our success was the hand held Dirt Devil. In 1991 we took the company public and my stock was worth about $40 million.

Another fairly good investment was Citizens National Bank in Naples, Florida. I had been playing golf with Joe Godfrey an ex-Vice President of General Motors. Joe said they were planning to put together a group in Naples of 30 investors at $100,000 each to raise $3 million. It was interesting because Barnett Bank had purchased Citizens National but did not make any provision about reserving the name. So we had a running start by naming the bank Citizens National Bank and opening in the same building they had been in before selling to Barnett. A lot of the customers didn't even know the old bank had been sold. As the bank grew they needed more capital and came back to the original investors twice. Each time I took the maximum amount I could. My 3.3% grew to about 4.4% which made me the largest stockholder. I had $350,000 invested in 1990 when we sold to SouthTrust. My investment brought two and a half million.

Ray Rossman, my banker friend who started Midwest Bank & Trust in Cleveland, came to Florida and started Island Bank on Marco Island. Naturally I was one of the stockholders. We sold that one to SouthTrust and made out fairly well.

In 1990 I invested in another great idea which, like the Phytofarms, turned out to be a loser. It was Indoor Fairways, a virtual golf course featuring many famous courses. You could play Pebble Beach, Pinehurst and places like that. When you hit the golf ball off the practice tee it went through a couple of infrared screens which measured the velocity and the spin. The computer measured your shot very accurately including slices and hooks. You could play a game of golf inside in the Winter in Cleveland. But we never could make any money with it. We finally folded the company and I lost about half a million.

At that point Mal Mixon and I decided to form a venture capital company which we called MCM Capital. We brought in Mark Mansour, a CPA and son of our attorney, Ernie Mansour, to run the company and sort through investment opportunities.

The first investment we bought through MCM was Wilshire Corporation, which had about $55 million in annual sales. Wilshire's main product was a soft drink dispenser used for colas at fast food chains like McDonald's and Burger King. Wilshire had a deal with Coca-Cola which was paying for half of their research and precluded sales to Pepsi. We pulled out of the deal with Coke so we could do our own research. That cost us some of the Coke business but we expanded in other areas, making up for the lost sales volume. After a few years we sold the company at a nice profit.

The next investment, in June 1992, was Cencor which provides businesses with temporary workers. A write up in Crain's Cleveland Business about this purchase described it as follows:

"Seeing Messrs. Mixon and Callahan in a deal together is sort of like seeing a lot of birds over one spot on the ocean. It's normally a sure sign of great fishing below."

We acquired Cencor as a result of an estate tax problem of the principal shareholder of Cencor's parent company which was on the New York Stock Exchange. Nancy Taber had set up about twelve offices for the company in Ohio. When the owner of the bulk of the company's stock died, his heirs needed to sell off parts of the company to pay the inheritance tax. So we bought the Ohio operations and got Nancy Taber to run the company. I knew from experience that hiring temporary workers is a good way to find out if the worker is any good before you make a commitment. About 30% of temporary workers become full time employees which is all right with the temp company because they charge a hiring fee. I always tell people looking for a job to go to a temp service company. That way you get to try out a job before you decide if you really want to work there long term. So it works well for the employer and employee. A public company in the same field was doing a roll-up and offered us a price we could not turn down. The result was another nice gain.

In 1994 we bought AccuSpray which developed a new type of low-pressure spray paint gun. It doesn't use as much paint in the process as other spray guns and you get a high finish. We tried to sell it to people repairing cars. One problem we ran into was trying to get paint sellers to sell the spray gun. They were not too interested in a spray gun that caused less paint to be used. However we were able to sell to Chrysler and also to home decorating and contract painting people. The company has proceeded to develop a line of airless products to expand the line. Most recently it has made great strides in the home paint and decorating segment becoming a supplier to Sherwin Williams, America's #1 paint company. In several years I am confident we will turn a good profit on AccuSpray.

Later in 1994 we bought R. J. Lee, an electron microscope company. They have combined the electron microscope with the computer and were able to sell the units for about $100,000 each.

In 1996 we acquired CV Materials which makes frit that is used to put a baked enamel finish on appliances like refrigerators and washing machines. That business is way down from what it was a few years back. Another product line is special frits used for lubricating dies for steel companies.

We also bought RockTron which is in the sound reproduction business. It's products are used by some of the better musical groups including Garth Brooks.

A start-up investment in 1996 was NeuroControl which has been developing an electrical device utilizing a technology called "functional ventrical stimulators" to make it possible for paraplegics and others to move their upper extremities and conduct their toilet functions without assistance. We think this has great potential and has recently gained FDA approval.

In 1997 we got involved with Dick Cooper who owns a coal mine. Dick needed equipment to wash the coal thereby lowering the sulfur content and making it more marketable. So we purchased the equipment for a part interest in the coal mine.

In 1998 we formalized our new venture capital company which we named MCM Capital. At this point MCM Capital has two purchases. In November 1998 we invested in One Source which provides nationwide repairs to CAT Scan and MRI equipment. In December 1998 we acquired Am Rep which has janitorial supplies.

Over many years of investing I am frequently asked, "How do you figure out what stocks to buy?" I think it is important to keep the portfolio fairly small, not more than 12 or 15 different companies. With my own company we would naturally get to know our suppliers and customers. The ones that were very confident about their own company and were investing in it seemed to be attractive to me. That's the reason I bought into companies like Exxon, ATT Labs, Monsanto, DuPont and Minnesota Mining and Manufacturing. Some companies, like Huntington, I was asked to go on the board and that way learned a lot about the company. I bought Citicorp when it was down to $10 a share because I didn't think the government would let a large bank like that go bankrupt. I sold it at $138 a share.

I tend to hold stocks for the long term because of the capital gain tax. The longer you hold the longer you postpone having to pay the tax. I try to avoid companies that are paying a dividend for two reasons. One, I don't want to pay the high tax on the dividend. Two, I prefer the company reinvest the earnings so the stock will go up in value over time. I used to have about 25% of my stock investment in what I called gambling stocks. Those are the more risky investments that had the potential to go up quite a bit. Now that I am in investment banking I consider that my gambling and the stock market is a place to park the money until I find an attractive company to buy.

10

One major virtue of telling the truth is you don't have to keep track of what you say.

Philanthropy

There are several ways in which a person can make a contribution to society. Among them are providing for a family, building a company that provides quality employment, goods and services and, the subject of this chapter, donations of time and money for worthy causes.

I have always felt that it is important to give of your time and finances in support of worthy causes for the betterment of the community. One of my first experiences was in 1960 when my son Joe was in the Boy Scouts. Because the Boy Scouts get some funding from the United Way we were not allowed to raise funds from the general public, only from friends and relatives.

In Joe's scout troop I was asked to do the fund raising from the parents. The target amount per scout was $12 per year - *"A*

Buck a Month" - which was the unfunded amount per scout. My approach to the parents was, "Certainly you want to pay for your own son, don't you?" If they looked hesitant I would add the kicker. "If you feel you can not afford it, try to talk your son into raising the $12 by doing odd jobs for the neighbors." With that approach I managed to get almost 100% donations from our troop of about 20 families.

Some of the other troops were not doing as well and I was asked to teach the other troops how we did it. I found out they were just asking for donations without giving a reason or putting on any pressure. I had discovered two of the fundamentals of fundraising. One, explain the need. And two, ask for the amount of the donation.

The next year I was asked to be the Skyline District Treasurer. We continued to improve by identifying parent leaders in each troop and working with them on their salesmanship skills. Then we decided it would probably be easier and we could get more money if we got people to come to a dinner function. In the district I got a list of all the people who had donated and picked out all the names that were well enough off that they could afford $100 for a dinner. I knew some of the Browns football players and Cleveland Indians baseball players. They volunteered to be guest speakers at the dinners. In this way we were raising $10,000 to $12,000 each year in the Skyline District. After that anyone who contributed $500 was invited to a golf outing held at Canterbury Golf Club. Everyone paid there own way for the outing. At the beginning we would only have three or four foursomes. It was just a way to get Friends of Scouts together. The golf tournament has now grown to a citywide $60,000 to $70,000 fundraiser for the scouts. It all started with raising $12 per year from parents to support their son's scouting activities.

The next thing I got involved in was the **Boys Club.**

Ed and Ginny Ismond were neighbors in Daisy Hill and very active in Boys Club. They asked me to help with a new club to be started on Buckeye Road. I got involved because I felt the Boys Clubs actually got more bang for the buck than the Scouts in helping the inner city kids. They build gymnasiums, have sporting events and provide tutoring for all the kids that needed help with their school work. They really do a terrific job. It is now expanded to Boys and Girls Clubs.

Junior Achievement is another worthwhile organization that I supported during the period my children were in school. They have high school kids form a small company, make a product and go out and sell it. I liked supporting the JA's because it got kids to realize that being a businessman wasn't a bad thing. It gave them an idea of what it took to run a business and that it could be fun.

I spent several years as a Trustee for the Cleveland Boys Club and Junior Achievement.

Son Joe was going to Gilmour Academy. One of their fund raisers was the Gold Ticket, which at that time cost $100 for a chance to win $10,000. At one of the Gold Ticket meetings I met some of the people there and they asked me to get on the Board of Trustees. I soon found out they were running in the red about a quarter million dollars a year and they were two million dollars in debt. On top of that they didn't have the actual financial results of the previous year or a budget for the coming year. And they wanted to raise teacher's pay. I said I didn't understand how they could raise teachers' pay in the blind. I complained so much they made me Chairman of the Board.

The school had gotten into trouble when the number of Brothers from the Holy Cross who taught for free started going down. They had to be replaced with compensated teachers and nobody was doing anything about re-evaluating costs.

After we established budgets and got back in the black, the next thing I changed was fundraising. At that time the only fund raiser they had was the Gold Ticket Sale. I remember when I was first sold a ticket, I was told, "Just buy a Gold Ticket and you won't be bugged with any more fund raisers." I started a $2.5 million campaign to get rid of the debt. When this was done my focus shifted to an endowment fund. At that time the school only had about $65,000 while other schools that size had endowments of $15 to $20 million. After several years we started a $10 million Endowment Drive. Today Gilmour has $20 million in Endowment.

Around 1978, Bill Williams who was President of Republic Steel Company and Chairman of the Board of Marymount Hospital asked me to go on the Marymount Board. Bill told me that it would only be for three years unless the board offered me another 3 year term and I agreed to stay. So the max time on the board would be six years. He also told me that it would not take much of my time.

Sister Mary Camille was President of Marymount, a fairly small hospital of 200 beds in Garfield Heights, Ohio. It was really the center of activity in Garfield Heights, being one of the largest employers. It was run by nuns from Detroit, Sisters of St. Joseph, Third Order of St. Francis. This was a Polish order and the many Polish people of the community were very supportive of the hospital.

The board was made up primarily from the local community. Bill wanted to recruit board members with a stronger financial background. Tom Truedell was scheduled to become the first lay President as Sister Mary Camille was retiring and the board would be required to be more active.

I served my first three years and was asked to stay on for three more years and be Chairman. About this time the federal government became much more active in health care with their DRG's and other acronyms starting to put a lot of financial pressure on small hospitals.

We decided that the small Doctor's Office building attached to the hospital should be expanded to insure that we could maintain our bed occupancy. This worked very well as we continued to have a strong patient load. It was also decided that we could do a better job for the community if we built an assisted living facility on the property. To do this we had to form a holding company.

My six years were coming to an end and they asked me to serve on the holding company board starting in 1984.

So I continued on with Marymount until I was asked to go on the board of the Cleveland Clinic in 1990. I felt it would be a conflict of interest to be on both boards, so I left Marymount to join Cleveland Clinic. Subsequently Marymount was merged into the Cleveland Clinic Health System. So I have been on hospital boards continuously since 1978.

During this period I also went on the Board of the Cleveland Orchestra, which is generally ranked among the top three orchestras in the world. Having a good orchestra is important to Cleveland because it gets good publicity and helps attract good people to the corporations and doctors to Cleveland Clinic and University Hospital. The orchestra has a close relationship with the Cleveland Institute of Music in that some 25 to 30 members of the orchestra are graduates of the Institute and probably 75% of the teaching staff of the Institute are from the Cleveland Orchestra. My wife was on the Woman's Committee and suggested that I should get interested in the Cleveland Institute of Music. It was a fairly weak board from the standpoint of having people who understood finances. The people running the board had the idea that you should be a musician to be on the board. I helped organize the fund raising department of the Institute of Music and did some work on the budgets and controls. David Cerone has done a great job as President

Jack Breen, Chairman of the Board of Sherwin Williams, asked me if I would go on the board of John Carroll University. I told him I didn't need anymore to do but that I would serve for a while. So I spent a couple of years on the board of John Carroll.

My main activity now, as I write this in 1999, is with the Cleveland Clinic Foundation. Since joining the board in 1990 I have served on five different committees, including Chairman of the Budget Committee and the Management Information System Committee. In 1995 I was asked to serve as Chairman of the *Securing the 21st Century* campaign. This is a capital campaign to raise $225 million to support the construction of The Lerner Research and Education Institute, the Cleveland Clinic Eye Institute and the Cleveland Clinic Taussig Cancer Center.

Bill Conway had been head of the Development Committee. He hired William Grimberg, an outstanding fund raising professional, to be Chairman of the Department of Institutional Advancement. We met together and agreed to start off by getting the "in house" people at the hospital involved. When that phase concluded in September 1997 we had raised $54 million from employees, professional staff and trustees. By going "in house" first gave us time to put our story together as to why we needed to raise the money and map out our strategy. My basic approach to fund raising is to make lists evaluating how much to ask from each person and then making person to person calls on prospective donors. You have to control the list so that each prospect on the list is only approached and developed by one person on the fund raising staff. At this point we have raised a total of about $160 million and I don't see any reason why we can't raise the balance by 2002 which is the closure of the campaign.

One question I run into with some people is, "Why does the clinic want to get so big?" My answer is that we just want to keep doing what we set out to do in the first place which is take care of the sick, do research to find the cause and cure of diseases and train those who serve. Most people did not realize that Cleveland Clinic was a nonprofit because they had not been active in fund raising. Because the Clinic has been so successful in the past with research it has run out of room for all the projects that it would like to do. Drug companies and others want to give us money to do research but we don't have the facilities. Every nook and cranny in the basements are used and the research facilities are scattered all over. Research is leading to exciting potentials in the fields of immunology and genetics. There are also technical breakthroughs for minimal invasive surgery using fiber optic television and small surgical tools. We have over 10,000 visiting doctors a year come in to see procedures. About 500 students from Ohio State take their last two years of medical school at the Cleveland Clinic and they need better facilities. The bottom line is the Cleveland Clinic has been so successful at what it does, the demand for it to do still more has outstripped the facilities available. So the capital campaign is very much needed.

Other than contributing my time I have also made sizable donations for worthy causes. I made a $5 million donation to The Callahan Center for Radiation Oncology and Robotics, which is part of the Cleveland Clinic, for the purchase of the Cyberknife. The Cyberknife is a unique merger of several leading-edge technologies, allowing linear accelerator beams to be focused on one point, the tumor or cancer. In this way only the focal point gets the full power of the beams and the surrounding areas are not damaged.

I gave a million dollars to the Cleveland Orchestra and endowed a chair there with an additional quarter million. At the Cleveland Institute of Music I endowed the Presidents Chair for one million. Mal Mixon and I donated a half million each to endow an Entrepreneurship Chair at Case Western Reserve University.

Looking back on my philanthropic activities, I started with the Boy Scouts, the Boys Clubs, Junior Achievement and Gilmour Academy primarily because my children were involved. As I got familiar with what was required for fund raising for nonprofit groups I started looking around at what were the important institutions in town that could use my help. That led to my long involvement with the hospitals, first Marymount and then Cleveland Clinic. And I also thought having a first rate Orchestra was important to making Cleveland attractive to corporate and medical executives and employees.

11

Shoot for the Pin!

Golf

Figure 88   At a company golf outing I was "hustled" into a gin game.

I always said I had three vices – the three G's. I drink gin. I play gin. And I play golf. Always told ● my wife she had no complaints as long as I didn't add the fourth G – girls.

My first exposure to golf was caddying for my Dad at Springbrook Country Club in Lima, Ohio when I was about 14 years old. A particularly memorable moment was getting hit on the chin by the first bounce of a drive Dad hit on the first hole at Spring Brook. I still have a scar on my chin from that drive and, yes, we did finish the round. A good lesson in perseverance. (Would you be able to keep playing while your young son is carrying your clubs and holding a handkerchief on his bleeding chin.)

In High School I played on the School Golf Team if I was not playing baseball. By playing on the school team we got to play the course at Shawnee Country Club. None of our team were members at any club. I had a golfing nickname of "Byron" because Byron Nelson was winning a lot of tournaments in those days.

While in the Navy, I played a couple times on the nine-hole course at the Sub Base in New London while on the K-1. Once with Dave Leighton, Class '46, we played at the Army-Navy Club in Washington DC while working for Rickover. On weekends while living in Acton, Massachusetts I used to drive 60 miles north of Boston to play a public course by myself at 6:00 AM. On one early morning outing by myself I made a double eagle with a drive and a three wood. Only time I made a double eagle and there were no witnesses.

When we moved to Cleveland in 1958, Fred Lennon and everybody in town played golf. Our suppliers, customers and distributors all played a lot of golf. I started playing the company league, nine holes one evening a week at Bratenahl Country Club; In 1960 I got serious and joined the Chagrin Valley Country Club. Walt Houston and I played quite a few rounds at Chagrin. When I started there I couldn't break 120

Figure 89   L-R, Walt Houston, Dale King & Chuck King make up one of my favorite foursomes.

and I tended to slow down a foursome. In about a year I was shooting under 90 and not holding people up on the golf course.

I found that playing golf was a great way to learn about people and make friends. You can learn a lot about a person on a golf course and I always tried to play golf with a potential distributor or a potential manager. You can spot good and bad personality traits on the golf course. The friends and customers I've made on the golf course are too numerous to count, but I have made an abbreviated list.

At Pepper Pike some of my favorite golf buddies have

*Figure 90   The Memorial Tournamet 1985 Pro-AM L-R: Mike Reid,
John Hipolit, Joe Callahan, Charles Rini & Steve Albrecht.*

been John Collinson, Julien McCall, Roy Gentles, Bob Healy, Dale King, Chuck King, Jerry McDonough and Bill Cosgrove.

At Canterbury I have enjoyed playing with Ernie Mansour, Nick Di Cicco, Tony Di Santo and Fred Di Santo.

Some of our golfing distributors and members of the corporate team have been Ed Holt, Bill Cosgrove, Bill Wilson, Bill Krevling, Tom Johnson, Bob Clark, Tom Read, Bob Jennings, Fred Brunk, Jack Cadagan, Dan McMonagle, Bob Crum, Bob Fouke, Hayden Fouke, Wolf Ast, Dave Cheetham, Jim Melas and Karl Kaimer.

I've played in numerous Pro-Ams. Three were particularly memorable. In 1985 we won the Memorial at Muirfield in Dublin, Ohio playing with Mike Reid. In 1986 we won the

Dispatch photo b)

Corey Pavin uncorks drive

Pro-am appearance rewards sub

Mike Reid stepped in for George Burns and led the last group off No. 10 tee in Tuesday's Memorial pro-am at Muirfield Village Golf Club. Five-plus hours later, Reid and Co. had lapped the field, finishing with a best-ball score of 17-under-par 55 to defeat Tom Purtzer's team by a stroke.

Reid's teammates were John Hipolit, F.J. Callahan, Charles Rini and Steve Albrecht.

Pros played for score if they wanted. The best rounds were by Mark O'Meara and Jim Thorpe, each with a 5-under-par 67. Ray Floyd, the 1982 Memorial champion, shot 68.

Reid earned $1,250. O'Meara and Thorpe earned $1,125 each.

★ ★
The last team off the course yesterday, playing with pro Mike Reid, won the pro-am with a 17-under total, John Hipolit, F.J. Callahan, Charles Rini and Steve Albrecht were the other team members.

Figure 91   Played the Memorial at Muirfield every year they had a Pro-Am. In 1985 with John Hipolit, Charles Rini and Steve Albrecht won the Memorial Pro-AM at Muirfield with a 17 under par.

Thursday, February 27, 1986
The Miami Herald   5D

Kratzert team wins

The winning pro-am team was Bill Kratzert, Tom Holton, Joe Callahan, Bob Burkett and Walt Schaub with a 20-under-par 52. Joey Sindelar was the low pro with a 65.

6D   The Miami Herald / Thursday, February 27, 1986   5

Kratzert team wins

The winning pro-am team was Bill Kratzert, Tom Holton, Joe Callahan, Bob Burkett and Walt Schaub with a 20-under-par 52. Joey Sindelar was the low pro with a 65.

Figure 92   In 1986 with Kratzert, Tom Holton, Bob Burkett and Walt Schaub won with a 20 under par 52

Honda Pro AM playing with Billy Kratzert. And in 1993 I shot a 71, my first and only under par round, while playing with Mark O'Meara in the Honda. We took third place. You should understand that in pro-ams they move all the white tees up so the holes are short, The par 3's all play at 130 to 150 yards and the par 4's are about 340 to 380 yards..

Some of the other Pros I recall playing with are Gary Player, Donna White, Sally Little, Peter Jacobsen, Bruce Lietzke, Marlene & Ray Floyd, D. A. Weibring, Chip Beck, Ian Woosman, Jay Brewer, Ken Brown, John Jacobs and Ben Smith.

On June 13, 1967 I had my first hole-in-one. It was at Landerhaven, hole #8, 178 yards with a 5 iron. We were playing a nine hole match in the Company League and my opponent for the night was Earl "Squirrel" Shufflebarger. When we left the 7th hole I had him one down and he said "I'm going to get you. I'm going to beat you on the next two holes and win the match." When I got on the 8th, I noticed that the pin was cut to the right side of the green and the tee markers were set to the right side of the tee. Trees were close to the right and my natural shot was a slight hook so I couldn't shoot at the flag. All I could do was try to draw the ball to the center of the green and hope I could 2 putt it for a par. The shot was hooking toward the center of the green and not even headed at the pin. When it hit, it bounced hard right, ran to the pin and went in. I would rather be lucky than good. I said to Squirrel, "How are you going to beat a one?"

My second hole-in-one was on November 6, 1968 from the Blue tee of Hole #9 on Pinehurst #2 Course, a shot of 190 yards. I was playing Frank Lowe. We were playing "do's or don'ts", double on birdies, quadruple on eagles. I was down 3. I had a good score going and decided I would lay up rather than getting in a lot of trouble going for the green. The

Figure 93   Honda Pro-Am 1986. I'm in the green sweater. To my left
are Walt Schaub, Billy Kratzert, Bob Burkett and Tom Holton.

foursome ahead waved us through. I took out my four iron, came over the top of the ball and knocked it on the ground, running between the trees over the pine needles. The ball reached the left edge of the left front trap, somehow ran through the trap, made a big arc across the green and went in the hole. Never off of the ground!

Frank and I had been playing for about five days and he had yet to win a nine. This shot evidently disturbed him because after his drive on ten he broke his driver in half. He continued to do this until he ran out of clubs and we headed in. I did not bother to turn in this hole-in-one to the pro shop.

My third hole-in-one was at Pelican Bay in Naples Florida on March 25, 1981 on hole #16, 148 yards with a seven wood. I finally made a true hole-in-one with one bounce and in.

The observers were all from Mayfield Country Club. They were Dale King, Rollie Carlson and Mike Bowden.

My fourth hole-in-one was again a seven wood at 180 yards, one bounce and in at #4 at Mayfield Country Club in the Ronald McDonald Pro-Am. Don Padgett, the Pro at Firestone Country Club, was in our group and it was the first hole in one he had ever seen. He said, "Aren't you excited?" And I answered, "What's there to be excited about? That's my fourth." The others in our group were Jim Boland, Eddie Crawford and Jack Breen. We were rained out on the second nine, but won the abbreviated tournament.

My fifth hole-in-one was made at Quail Creek, hole #7, 137 yards on May 1, 1987 with a seven iron. The month before I was playing with my lawyer, Ernie Mansour, out in Phoenix, Arizona at the Goodyear Course. My partner, Bob Clark, had just hit a shot about a foot from the cup on a par three. Ernie followed Bob to the tee and made a hole-in-one to beat us. I said "Ernie, how many is that?" He replied "Five." I acknowledged that he had me down by one. When I was teeing it up for #7 at Quail Creek, I said, 'This is my chance to catch you." When I made it we were tied at five apiece.

My sixth came at Indian Wells, California at hole #6 on January 30, 1989, 120 yards with a nine iron. I was one ahead of Ernie again. Unfortunately Ernie knocked another one in on #4 at Canterbury in April of 1989 and we were back in a tie at six apiece. This is the only hole-in-one competition between two close friends I know of that's up to the rarefied number of six.

In the appendix I have listed over 100 golf courses I have played. Many of these I have played many times. In all, I probably played over 1000 rounds of golf, figuring that from

Figure 94   Hole-in-Ones #s 1 & 2.

Figure 95   My 4ᵗʰ Hole-in-One with Fred Lennon and Don Padgett.

1965 to 1995 I played at least 35 rounds a year. Assuming 1000 rounds at 4 hours a round, I have only spent 4000 hours playing golf. Since there are 8760 hours in a year, I have actually spent less that half a year in my 75 years playing golf. If you consider that in 75 years I have lived 657,000 hours, then 4000 hours of golf is only 0.6% of my life. That comes out to less than 9 minutes a day. That's less time than I spend getting dressed or talking to the cat. So obviously I did not neglect my family for golf, when it took such a minuscule part of my total time on earth.

When I made my 4th hole in one at the Ronald McDonald Pro-Am at Mayfield Country Club in June 1981, some of my friends followed me home tooting their horns.

Mary came out and exclaimed, "What the heck is going on?"

My friends said, "Joe made his fourth hole-in-one in the tournament today."

Mary said, "What's the big deal about that?'

When told that a hole-in-one only happens about every 10,000 shot, Mary's rejoinder was, "Well in that case, as much as he plays, he should have more than four."

Actually she was right. Again assuming I've played 1000 rounds with an average score of 84. I have taken 84,000 shots to achieve 6 hole-in-ones. That's only one every 14,000 shots.

When people have asked me how I was able to make six hole-in-ones, I answered, "It's no secret. I always shoot for the pin."

Some of my favorite golf lore.

1. Lee Trevino said, when he had hit his second shot on the green about 40 feet from the cup, "I'm on the dance floor but I can't hear the music."

2. Another Trevino saying: "Feed me Alpo. I'm playing like a dog."

3. And yet another Trevino classic: "Every day I'm playing worse. And today I'm playing like tomorrow."

4. Not many people know the origin of the word "sandbagger" to indicate a cheater in golf. Early golf courses were near the ocean and people who played golf often also sailed. In sailing races it has always been against the rules to have movable ballast because shifting it from side to side can help right the boat, helping the more vertical sails catch more air and therefore go faster. People who carried sandbags were called sandbaggers and considered cheaters in sailing races. Thus the term sandbagger for one who cheats or takes unfair advantage in golf.

5. The French have various sayings in golf that differ from ours such as "toupee" for "divot". Another term they use is "danielowe" when a golf ball is left short right on the lip of the cup. The story behind this strange name is that at one time there was a French Bishop named Danielowe who at age 76 took up with an 18-year-old mademoiselle. A scandal ensued when he died in bed just as he was attempting to consummate the affair. The great publicity from this event led, in typical French humor, to call a putt that almost reached the hole a "danielowe".

I will end this chapter with Forgan's Creed which expresses the reason golf has meant so much to me through the years.

What is Golf?

*It is a science - the study of a lifetime, in which you may
exhaust yourself but never your subject.*

*It is a contest, a duel or a melee, calling for courage,
skill, strategy and self control.*

It is a test of temper, a trial of honor, a revealer of character.

*It affords a chance to play the man (or woman),
and act as the gentleman (or lady)!*

*It means going into God's out-of-doors, getting close to nature.
Fresh air, exercise, a sweeping away of the mental
cobwebs, genuine recreation of the tired tissues.*

It is a cure for care, an antidote to worry.

*It includes companionship with friends, social intercourse,
opportunity for courtesy, kindliness and
generosity to an opponent.*

It promotes not only physical health but moral force.

Forgans Creed
by David Forgan

Figure 96   Forgan's Creed.

12

*Not all problems are solvable. Learn to live with the
problems you cannot solve.*

Parting Thoughts

In this chapter I will make some miscellaneous comments
about things that just didn't get included in the other chapters.

Thinking back to my time with Rickover, some people
questioned why he wasted the money on the Seawolf reactor that
was cooled by sodium. The Nautilus and subsequent nuclear
powered ships have used pressurized water plants. In hindsight
the Seawolf was unnecessary. But at the time both designs were
new technology and we weren't sure that either would work. They
were designed in parallel in hopes that at least one would work.
So in my opinion that criticism of Rickover is unjustified.

One of my early insights into what became the frenzied merger
and acquisition period of the 1980's occurred with Tappan
Company and my introduction to Carl Ichan.

In 1981 Dick Tappan, Chairman of the Tappan Company, came down to Naples, Florida to ask me to go on Tappan's Board of Directors. After a short discussion I agreed to accept.

Within two years we had sold the air conditioning business and were getting the objectives of the Gas Stove and Cabinet divisions clarified. Profits were turning around and we felt we were making progress. Tappan's stock was selling at 11 to 12 dollars per share and we became an early take over target of Carl Ichan.

Carl bought a large block of Tappan stock and by cumulative voting of his shares managed to place himself on the board. When he arrived at his first board meeting he announced that he had a buyer for the Company at $15 per share. All of a sudden Tappan was for sale even though we had no plans to sell. Rather than submit to the hostile takeover from Ichan, we searched around and found a Swedish company, Electrolux, which bought the company for $18 per share. Later Ichan became a large player in this type of transaction. One of his takeovers made him Chairman of TWA.

Since Swagelok is privately owned we never had to face takeover threats. But there were other predators we had to defend against. A minor nuisance was the OSHA (Office of Safety and Health Administration) auditors. Our safety standards have always been so high that I am sure it was a frustrating experience for them to find anything to write up on us. They were never a problem and I was actually disappointed in the quality of people the government would send to our plants. Their unkempt appearance was a violation of our own dress code for our employees.

A major nuisance however was caused by a scam that is perpetrated on many companies like Swagelok. The anti-trust laws are so complicated that practically any business could be construed to be in violation of some part. "Unfair competition" could be the result of 1) lowering prices, 2) raising prices or 3) refusing to do either 1 or 2 under certain market conditions. Consequently there are lawyers who will file an anti-trust lawsuit against a company expecting to settle out of court and collect a big contingency fee.

In 1980 such a suit was filed against Swagelok by Joe Allioto, the ex mayor of San Francisco. Fortunately we had Ernie Mansour as our lead attorney. Ernie led us through the case and after a five year battle we received a directed verdict from the Federal Judge in New Orleans. Our costs were over $5 million, but we won.

Now on to some more pleasant topics.

When we moved from Acton, Massachusetts in 1958 to Cleveland, we bought an old house in Chagrin Falls at 64 Maple Street. Right across the street from us lived Cliff and Alice Nelson. In the Spring of 1959 while I was cutting the grass in the front yard, Cliff called over and asked, "Do you play tennis?"

I said yes and we started playing on the school courts at Chagrin High School. We decided to enter the Northeast Ohio Tennis League. In 1962 we won the doubles championship in the league. This may seem like quite an accomplishment but it really wasn't. Hardly anyone was playing tennis at this time. When we would go to cocktail parties, our "friends" would wave to us with a limp wrist and say "Oh here are the tennis players. La De Da."

Ten years later tennis regained its popularity and they were all playing. Cliff and I continued to play quite a bit until he and Alice moved to Atlanta. The moral of the story is that just

Figure 97   With Cliff Nelson, my tennis partner.

because you are not marching in step does not mean you are not ahead of the game.

An activity that I have enjoyed in Florida is sailing. Our first residence in Florida was a condominium in Admiralty Point in 1979. Admiralty Point is on Doctors Pass in Naples. They had some boat docks for the condo owners across the road but they were all taken. I put my name on the waiting list. About a year later I received notice that a dock was available for me and I had 30 days to put my boat in the dock. I had not planned to buy a boat until I got the notice. I quickly found a used FMC sloop, about 25' long with a six-foot centerboard and one-cylinder eight-horsepower diesel engine. I named the boat *Golf Widow* in honor of my wife. Mary had

Figure 98   On Golf Widow

insisted that I get the boat in hopes I wouldn't spend so much time on the golf course.

We replaced this boat with a Cape Dory 30' Motorsailor sloop, 43 horsepower 6-cylinder diesel in 1990 named *Golf Widow II.* Outside of running aground two times, our boating has been pretty routine.

I was lucky enough in October of 1994 to ride the USS OHIO SSBN-726 to 100 miles off Cape Canaveral and observe the firing of a ballistic missile 4500 miles to Ascension Island off the coast of Africa. This trip was arranged by Captain "Chip" Seymour who is head of Development at the Naval Academy. As we came ashore Chip and I went to a bar where we did some brain storming about ways to improve fund raising at the Academy, especially in the area of Endowment.

I told him with the Alumni lists he had that included the jobs and titles of all Naval Academy graduates it should be

Figure 99   Golf Widow II tied up at my dock in Naples, 1999.

easy to raise funds. The first thing was to convince the graduates of the need. Everyone thinks that all the money to run the Academy is furnished by the government. I suggested several ideas for doing this and then laid out an idea for a Challenge Campaign that could develop into an annual tradition. My class, 1946, was having its 50th reunion in 1995. During the war we had compressed the four years into three and graduated in June 1945. But we were still the class of 46.

My suggestion was that we list the most successful graduates in civilian jobs and see if we could get 15 to 29 to donate a total of $500,000. Then we would challenge the rest of the class to match our half million to make a $1 million Endowment Gift for our 50th anniversary. Once accomplished, I suggested that the Class of '46 would then challenge all past and succeeding classes to raise $1 million for the Endowment Fund in honor of their 50th anniversary.

Our Class completed its goal in 1997 and this is now an on-going program.

Figure 100   Five submariners from the Class of '46 before the 50th reunion. L-R: Ed Holt, Charlie Woods, Joe Callahan, Frank King, Chuck Griffith.

In the unfinished business department, I am still trying for my 7th hole-in-one. The odds are tougher now as I'm not as limber as before. But considering that I had a right shoulder rotator cuff operation in '85, left hip replaced in '87, lower aorta repair in '96 and right hip replace in '97 I've earned the nickname of the bionic man. I can sometimes get it close to the cup on a 170-yard par three with my best driver shot. Hope springs eternal.

The title of these memoirs, *Shoot for the Pin*, expresses not only my golf philosophy but also my approach to life in general. An objective, once determined, should be pursued relentlessly and without compromise. This has been my approach in business, fund raising and golf. In the presentation I made to all new employees at Swagelok I warned against expediency, the short sighted, unprincipled approach. I said, *We will stick to our policy of fairness and not be governed by expediency.* And that's what we have done. We "shoot for the pin." Or as Sweet Talking Brown might say when questioned about his blunt statement, "The hell you ain't!" [page180]

To close this miscellany, I must recount the addition we had to our family on Halloween last year (1998). We had noticed a stray seal point Siamese cat that appeared around our house for about a week. Whenever we made any move towards it, it ran for cover and disappeared.

On Halloween Day it was so weak that it let us pick him up. He was nothing but skin and bones, weighing only five pounds. We named him "Boo" after a ghost we had in the front yard. We took Boo to Frank Coy, a vet, and had him checked out. His blood work showed many poor readings. With good care Boo now weighs 11 pounds and looks great. He has regained his confidence, jumping up on my lap whenever the mood strikes.

Barbara had a cat when we were married. However it was lost while being boarded at her vet during the time we were in Florida. We feel God sent us Boo as a replacement.

Figure 101   Boo in his usual place.

APPENDIX
A

Highlights in the Life of

Francis Joseph Callahan, Jr.

July 8, 1923	Born in Lima, Ohio
May, 1941	Graduated from St. Rose High School
Spring, 1942	Accepted to Coast Guard Academy
July 22, 1942	Reported to US Naval Academy
June 6, 1945	Commissioned Ensign US Navy, graduating from the Academy 77th out of a starting class of 1250
June 30, 1945	Married Mary Krouse at St. Rose Church in Lima, Ohio
July 8, 1945	Reported to Naval Air Station in Jacksonville, Florida

August 6, 1945	Reported aboard USS Cuttlefish (SS 171) in New London, CT
August 27, 1945	Reported to Submarine School, New London, CT
December 22, 1945	Graduated Submarine School
February 14, 1946	Reported aboard USS Grouper (SS 214)
December 27, 1946	Birth of first son, Francis Joseph Callahan III at Faulkner Hospital in Boston, MA
January 15, 1947	Assigned to MIT for courses in Naval Electronics
June 6, 1948	Promoted to Lieutenant JG
September 24, 1948	Graduated from MIT with the Degree of Bachelor of Science in Electrical Engineering
October 4, 1948	Reported aboard USS Volador (SS 490)
August 26, 1950	Detached from Volador and reported aboard USS Sterlet (SS 392)
February 28, 1951	Reported aboard USSK-1 (SSK-1) Primary duty Operation Officer, Communication Officer and Electronic Repair Officer.
July 31, 1952	Qualified for Command of Submarines

November 29, 1952	Interview with Rickover - Approval for Masters in Advanced Nuclear Engineering received on December 17, 1952.
April 7, 1953	Daughter, Cornelia Callahan, born at Faulkner Hospital in Boston, MA
June 8, 1953	Report to MIT
August 1954	Report to Bureau of Ships, Washington DC
February 28, 1956	Birth of son, Timothy John Callahan
April 1, 1957	Promoted to Lt. Commander
August 24, 1957	Submitted resignation from US Navy
January 6, 1958	Honorable Discharge from US Navy and accepted membership in US Navy Reserve.
October 1958	Promoted to President of Nupro Corporation
December 1959	Promoted to Executive VP of Crawford Companies.
April 14, 1961	Promoted to Commander USNR-R
July 1, 1961	Appointed Commanding Officer, NRRC 4-8
July 1, 1966	Promotion to Captain USNR-R
June 13, 1967	First Hole-in-One at Landerhaven hole 18.
May 1, 1976	Transferred to Retired Reserve

July 1, 1980	President of Crawford Fitting Company
July 8, 1983	Retired from Navy Reserve
October 10, 1996	Married Barbara Savage at Gilmour Academy Chapel
August 1, 1999	Chairman of Board, Swagelok

APPENDIX
B

Favorite Golf Courses I Have Played

(*Past Member,   **Current Member)

Cleveland Area

Chagrin Valley*
Kirtland**
The Country Club**
Canterbury
Shaker Heights
Pleasant Hills
Fowler Mills
Grantwood
Highland
Twin Lakes
Berkshire Hills
Oak Knolls
Auburn Springs
Boston Hill
Avon Lake

Mayfield*
Pepper Pike**
Firestone*
Aurora
Lakewood
Manakiki
Beachwood
Elyria
Portage
Acacia
Bratenahl
Walton
Landerhaven
Tanglewood
Sharon

Naples Area

Pelican Bay*
Eagle Creek
Naples National**
Royal Poinciana**(2)
Flamingo Lely
The Island Club
Spanish Wells
Naples Golf & Beach
Bay Colony
Lely Palms
Grey Oaks
Quail Run
Fox Fire

Palm River
Quail Creek*(2)
Audubon (2)
Vinyards
Windstar
Bears Paw
Bonita Bay
Habiscus
Wilderness
Moorings
Imperial
Old Florida

Other US Courses

Pine Valley
Cypress Point
Crystal Downs
Baltusrol (2)
Double Eagle
Chicago Golf Club
Butler Country Club
PGA West
Martha's Vineyard
Golden Horsehoe
Submarine Base, New London
Newport Country Club
New Orleans Country Club

Pebble Beach
Augusta National
Hilton Head (8)
Muirfield
Texas A&M
Inverary
Eagle Trace
Weston
Indian Wells
Army-Navy
Amelia Island
Pinehurst (5)
Mid Pines

Other US Courses (Continued)

Sea Island Georgia (4)
Louisiana Country Club
Country Club of NC
The Club at Long Leaf
Atlanta National Country Club

Nantucket
Aiken, GA
Whispering Pines
Canyon Club
Bermuda Dunes

Over Seas

Hawaii (6)
Puerto Rico (4)
Barbados (2)
England (2)

Australia (2)
St. Croix
St. Martens

Scotland:

St. Andrews (3)
Western Gales
Old Prestwich
Northern Gales
Royal Aberdeen
Aberdeen Muni
Glen Eagles (3)

Muirfield
Carnoustie
Turnberry (2)
Prestwich
Troon
Troon Muni

Index

Chicago Hull House Midgets 6
Chua, Chen Tong 197, 198
Citicorp 229
Citizens National Bank 226
Civilian Military Training Corps
    (CMTC) 5
Clancy, Tom 156
Clark, Bob 242, 246
Claytor, Rick 147, 149, 150, 171
Cleveland Boys Club 233
Cleveland Clinic viii, 53, 79, 81, 83,
    84, 235, 236, 237, 238
Cleveland Clinic Foundation 81, 84
Cleveland Clinic Taussig Cancer
    Center 236
Cleveland Indians 87
Cleveland Institute of Music 81, 84
Cleveland Orchestra 81, 82, 87
Coast Guard Academy 21, 22, 259
Code 500 156
Cohen, Al 115, 124
Collinson, John 242
Colquhoum, Dick 101
Combat Information Center 132
Computer Tomography 222
ComSubDevGroup II 120
ComSubDevGruII 159, 166
ComSubFlot6, Charleston, South
    Carolina 167
ComSubLant 119, 120, 122, 148,
    165, 168
Concord Hospital 52
Connie v, 28, 30, 51, 57, 58, 61, 69,
    70, 71, 72, 73
ConSubDevGroup II 119
Contract Bridge 19
Conway, Bill 236
Cooper, Dick 229
Cosgrove, Bill 205, 206, 242
Cowdrey, Roy 116
Coy, Frank 258
Crain's Cleveland Business 227

Crammer, Shannon 35
Crawford, Eddie 246
Crawford Fitting Company 262
Creighton 65
Crowther, Hubby 74
Crum, Bob 200
Cushing, Len 96
CV Materials 228

D

Daley, Bill 5
Danielowe 249
Davis, Noel 220
Dayton Chaminade 16
Del Coronado Hotel 114
diabetes 50, 80, 81
Diamond, Mrs. 11
Dibert, Sam 191
Dietzen, Bucky 35
Dill, Reese 183
Dirt Devil 225, 226
Distinguished Fellows Award 84
Dornick, John 18
Duggans 12
DuPont 229
Durbin, Margie 18

E

E&J 222, 224
Eastman Kodak 74
Eisenhower, Mamie 130
Electric Boat 114, 118, 127, 130,
    133, 141, 143, 147, 148, 149,
    150, 166, 167, 203
Electrolux 252
Endowment Fund vi, 234
Entrepreneurship Chair 238
Environmental Growth Control
    220
Essex Hotel 186
Euraneus, Carl 180

Evans, Whitney 222
Everest & Jennings 222
Executive MBA 80
Exxon 229

F

Falk, Englebert 3
Falk, Englebertha 3
Falk, Maxmillan 3, 12
Falk, Uncle Harry 8
Faulkner Hospital in Boston 260, 261
Favret, Andy 21, 48
Firestone Country Club 246
Fleet Ballistic Missile (FBM) Submarine Force vi
Fleet Ballistic Missile Submarines 164
fleet boat 132
Flick, Carol Ann 18
Floyd, Marlene & Ray 244
Forbes 186
Forgan's Creed 249, 250
Fort Benjamin Harrison 5
Fort Collins, Colorado 7
Fort Severn 31
Fouke, Bob 242
Fouke, Hayden 242
Frye, Elizabeth 3, 12
Frye, Frederick 3
Ft. Wayne Friars 6

G

Galileo 93
Gallagher, Bernie 175, 176, 188, 198
Gallagher, Mary Kay 175
Garotte, Mary Eliza 46
Gehrig, Lou 6
General Electric 134, 150
Gentles, Roy 242

Georgetown University 23
Gilmour 59, 69, 74, 86, 88, 233, 234, 238, 262
Ginny 61, 65, 67, 68
Glen Oak 69
Godfrey, Joe 226
golf v, viii, 16, 17, 23, 29, 90, 92, 154, 163, 165, 183, 192, 193, 206, 226, 232, 239, 240, 241, 242, 246, 248, 249, 254, 255, 256, 257, 263, 264
Golf Widow 255, 256
Golf Widow II 256
Goodyear Course 246
Goudsmit, Sam 162
Griffith, Chuck 257
Grimberg, William 236
Guppy 100, 120, 125

H

Haig, Durell 186
Halloran, Bernie 6
Hamilton, Noel 176
Hannafin, Pat 164
Hannah 71, 72
Hannon, Tommy 15
Harris Corporation 223
Harvard Medical School 50
Healy, Bob 242
Hillsdale College 217
Hipolit, John 242
Histerman, Catherine 3
hobos 9
Hoffman la Roche 196
Holden, William 113
hole-in-one 244, 245, 246, 247, 248, 257
Hollins College 70
Holt, Ed 202, 204, 242, 257
Holton, Tom 243, 245
Holy Cross 233

Nelson, Byron 240
Nelson, Cliff 254
NeuroControl 229
New London, Connecticut 21, 41,
    43, 49, 57, 69, 94, 99, 114,
    127
New York Celts 6
Newport Country Club 165
Newport, Kentucky 3, 12
Norton, Judy 26
Nuclear Products Company 172,
    174
Nupro 59, 152, 175, 176, 178, 179,
    186, 188, 191

O

Oak Ridge Tennessee 155, 178
O'Callaghan, Thomas 2
O'Connell, Henora 2
O'Connels 12
Office of Chief of Naval Operations
    (OP 31) 163
Ohio State 11, 28, 237
Ohio State Boxing and Wrestling
    Association 11
O'Keefe, Patrick 2
Olson, Nancy 113, 114
O'Meara, Mark 244
ONR - Brookhaven National Lab
    162
ONR - Code 162
ONR Seminar - Washington DC
    155
Operational Readiness Inspections
    104, 112
ordinance 160, 164
Orosz, Pat 87
osteoporosis 53
Oswego Giants 6

P

Pace, Stan 222
Padgett, Don 246, 247
paperless 208
Pavarotti 75
Pebble Beach 226
Pelican Bay 245
Pellegrinni, Bob 9, 18
Pennsylvania Railroad 9
Pentenberg, Louie 18
Pepper Pike Golf Course 183
Perquin, Franz 196
Peruvian Ambassador 128
Phytofarms of America 220
Pickerel 100
Pinehurst 226, 244
Player, Gary 244
pool parlor 19
Portsmouth Naval Shipyard 55, 99,
    100, 167
President's Chair 237
Public Television 75
Putnam, Captain Charles 95
Pyle, Ernie 18

Q

Quail Creek 246
Quantico Marines 27
Quatman, George 17
Quinn family 9
Quinn, John 18

R

Radar and Sonar School 50
Radar Picket Submarine 94, 95,
    96, 125, 132, 133
Rauch, Chuck 108
Read, Tom 191, 242
Reid, Mike 242
Republic Steel Company 234

T

Taber, Nancy 227
Talbot, Bud 224
Tantum Ergo 13
Tappan Company 251, 252
Tappan, Dick 252
Taylor, Don 113
Techmation 194
Technicare 221, 222, 225
Texas A & M 165
"The Log" 36
The World We Live In 119
Thompson, Howie 100, 101, 104, 120
Tim v, 51, 58, 59, 66, 69, 73, 74, 75, 78, 79, 80, 83, 87
Tinker, Alan 195
Tisdale, Chuck 108, 112
Tisdale, Robert 108
TJ 77, 78, 79, 85, 87
Toledo Paints 6
Tom 234
Toner, Catherine Mary 46
Trevino, Lee 249
Tricia 61, 62, 64, 65, 66, 67, 68, 85
Trinity College 47
Truedell, Tom 234
Truman, President Harry 127
Tube Fitters Manual 187
Tullibee Project 134
Tuscaloosa, Alabama 70
TWA 252

U

U.S. Submarine Force vi
Uncle John 1, 10
United States Naval Academy 31, 43
United Way 231

University of Alabama 70
University of Dayton 18, 20, 21, 27
University of Virginia 187
USS Arkansas 40
USS Cuttlefish (SS171) 49, 94
USS Grouper (SS214) 54, 132, 166
USS K-1 (SS K-1) 57, 115
USS New York 40
USS OHIO SSBN-726 255
USS Redfish 109
USS Seawolf (SSN 575) 143
USS Skylark 159
USS Sterlet (SS 392) 106, 107
USS Tang 117
USS Thresher (SSN-593) 159
USS Triton (SSRN 586) 117, 131
USS Volador (SS 490) 100, 109

V

Valley Forge 101, 103, 104
Van Dyke, John 188, 189
vertical integration 206
Vice Chief Naval Operations 168
Vietnam 60, 64, 65
VJ Day 49
Vladivostok 106

W

Walker China 152, 153
Walker, Johnny 194
Walsh, Jack 18
Warder, Admiral Freddie 147
Warner & Swasey 215
Washington Redskins 27
Weber, Bill 223
Weber, Mary 52
Weibring, D. A. 244
Weiss, Bronco 194, 196
Welch, Ray 96, 112

Wennerstrom, Earl 176
West Point 4, 21, 48
White, Donna 244
White, Dr. Priscilla 50, 58
Whitey Company 179
Whittle, Al 32
Why Not the Best 115
Wilkinson, Dennis 104, 105, 112, 129, 130, 141, 163
Wilkinson, Eugene P. (Dennis) 104, 168
Will 87, 88, 89
Williams, Barbara Joan 28
Williams, Betty 28
Williams, Beverly Jean 28
Williams, Bill 234
Williams, Deborah Kay 28
Williams, Donna Marie 28
Williams, Janet Rose 28
Williams, Ronald Lee 28
Williams, Tom 28
Wilshire Corporation 227
Wilson, Bill 175, 242
Wisconsin 3, 12
Wise, Adele 27
Wm. Paul Gallagher Post 5
Woods, Bets 116
Woods, Charlie 115, 116, 119, 125, 257
Woosman, Ian 244
World War II vi, 24, 41, 118, 164
Wouters, Luc 195

X

Xerox 74

Y

Yellowstone National Park 7
Young, R. J. 35

Z

Zachry, Dave 35
Zurich, Switzerland 90

Symbols

419 West McKibben Street 9
64 Maple Street 59, 253